CAPITALISM
AND
CHRISTIANS

Tough Gospel Challenges in a Troubled World Economy

by
Arthur Jones

Paulist Press
New York　Mahwah

Library of Congress Cataloging-in-Publication Data

Jones, Arthur, 1936–
    Capitalism and Christians: tough gospel challenges in a troubled world economy/by Arthur Jones.
      p.   cm.
    Includes bibliographical references.
    ISBN 0-8091-3345-8 (pbk.)
    1. Capitalism—Religious aspects—Christianity.   2. World politics—20th century. I. Title.
BRII5.C3J66   1992
261.8′5—dc20   92-26350
                                                         CIP

Published by Paulist Press
997 Macarthur Boulevard
Mahwah, New Jersey 07430

Printed and bound in the
United States of America

Dedication

*For my dear friend
(and mother-in-law)
Beatrice O'Brien
who truly knows
what money is for*

Foreword

I used to believe that our political perspectives determined our economic perspectives. Show us a New Deal liberal or someone still nostalgic for Adlai Stevenson, and we'd be able to make a shrewd guess about his or her degree of commitment to a free-market economy. I now believe I had it exactly backward, and that the way it goes in the "real world" is that our economic perspectives determine our political perspectives. Show us advocates of supply side economics or students of Milton Friedman and we could make an even shrewder guess about whom he or she supports in a presidential election. It's not so much, I've come to feel, our political allegiances that are the bottom line, as our economic commitments.

That's an inner feeling, and whatever else it does, it helps unmask our gut-level approach to life. There's an outer counterpart, however, of which we must be equally aware: certain events on the human scene can compel us to rethink all such matters. Sometimes "the facts" outrun our ability to fit them into our previously tidy schemes, and force us to reassessment.

In 1989, for example, with the freeing up of eastern Europe, it appeared that "socialism" had taken quite a beating and was retiring, not too gracefully, from the scene. In 1991, when Russia unraveled at the seams, it appeared that "communism" had met a similar fate. These empirically observable realities were followed by an assumption, far from empirically observable, that the upheaval had "proved" the superiority of capitalism as a way of life over all contenders.

Leaders in Russia, apparently acting on this premise, were suddenly hell-bent (the word is chosen carefully) to introduce a totally free market economy (with prices left to the determination of the market), even though those administering the transition had lived in a state-dominated economy all their lives and had not one iota of experience in administering alternatives. The only assured results so far (I write in February 1992) are a lot of increasingly hungry and frustrated people, for whom food and jobs remain illusory.

But things on the home front are not so tidy either. The economy of the nation where capitalism has had its greatest successes is in an unanticipated time of doldrums and decay. No one in public life has the ghost of a notion about how to restore confidence in the market, and various stop-gap proposals (a tax break for the middle class, a relaxation of the capital-gains tax for the wealthy) are widely acknowledged as offering little or no help in the long run. The refrain of the 1992 presidential campaign—"jobs, jobs, jobs"—is one to which the capitalist system in the United States is having great difficulty responding.

Even if the above scenario turns out to be overly pessimistic, and opposite consequences ensue, the issues that it raises need fresh scrutiny from "ordinary folk," i.e. those of us not trained in economics, fearful of emerging as a klutz in any discussion of economic issues, and yet realizing that it is economics that determines whether our ability to produce, market and sell will have sufficient vigor to provide us with food, clothing, and housing in the years ahead.

Christians who believe that the gospel has some things to say about food, clothing and housing have a special stake in this scrutiny and the kinds of responses it must elicit.

And this is where Arthur Jones comes in to offer help. His economics credentials are impressive. He has been

European Bureau Chief for *Forbes*, correspondent or contributing editor to such journals as the *Financial Times of London* and the *Washington Business Journal*, and he has written a number of books on the economy. His Christian credentials are impressive too. He has written for *The Catholic Star Herald*, *The Tablet*, and the *National Catholic Reporter*, of which he was editor-in-chief for five years. Although his own roots are incontrovertibly Catholic, he makes wise use of Protestant writings and pronouncements (and is even ecumenical enough to invite a Presbyterian to write the Foreword to this book). In addition—and maybe most important of all—he is clear and direct at all times, and blunt when necessary ("Though I love business, this book will strongly show that I don't like capitalism"). Mirrors are not part of his equipment as a writer on economics; reason, analysis, research, are. So no matter where the reader is coming from, it will be apparent where the author is coming from, and why. Clear gain for all.

It is not the purpose of the Foreword to summarize Arthur Jones' argument. He writes with a clarity that obviates such a necessity, and he even provides summaries of his own along the way. One of them is so clear and direct that it is worth reproducing here as a way of teasing potential readers to continue turning the pages.

> The cumulative charge to this point is that, measured against Christian precepts, first world capitalist activity . . . is (a) detrimental to the common good, (b) injurious to the planet, (c) but, worst of all, it promotes a false god, materialism, in the form of personal affluence and social "success."
>
> The four major worries that arise for the Christian are: (1) that the quest for personal affluence

contradicts what God expects us to do with creation, (2) as we lopsidedly share out of the world's wealth, we take essentials from the poor by demanding non-necessities for ourselves, (3) the ethos of capitalist materialism is smothering the voices of individuals, families and major Christian religions alike that oppose this materialistic ethos, its values and goals, and (4) there is an insidious attempt by capitalism's apologists to attribute Christian, or Judeo-Christian, values to this capitalistic materialism.

Should these "worries" seem groundless to readers, they are invited to study the text up to Chapter 7, where the above paragraphs appear, and then proceed under the author's direction to reflect on how to eliminate the causes for such worries.

*   *   *   *   *

When John Paul II's encyclical *Centesimus Annus* was released in 1991, North American readers will remember that certain neo-conservative theologians were able (by the simple and morally dubious act of breaking the embargo) to present a consistently pro-capitalist interpretation of *Centesimus Annus*. This was one-sided to say the least, and Arthur Jones presents us with copious materials from the encyclical that will help to set matters straight.

His division into capitalism "the good, the bad, and the ugly" enables him to say a few positive things along the way. His thesis that capitalism the "good" (i.e. business) is a good thing spoiled may draw some critique from the left, but the evidence produced to describe capitalism the "bad" and capitalism the "ugly" is overwhelming. Even if it were to be argued that committed individuals could "redeem" the system at this late date, the evidence suggests that the system has an unparalleled ability to destroy those who question it. Furthermore, when "greed" has been entrenched and blessed, as happened during the Reagan years, there are diminishing possibilities for change. And the free-swinging Chapter 6 on "plutocracy" (or government by the wealthy) will dispel any remaining naiveté.

Jones insists that Christians must live "counter-cultural" lives, and he offers some suggestions for doing so in the final chapters. Three examples show where the argument leads: (1) Christians must support debt-forgiveness for third world countries hopelessly mired in the financial demands of their first world creditors from which they cannot possibly escape, even with the best will in the world. (2) Churches need to make capital available (if necessary by borrowing on their paid-up real estate) for community development programs. (3) Steps must be taken to create worker-owned and worker-managed industries. No one of these is a "quick fix," but all such proposals deserve consideration and consequent action.

Arthur Jones takes seriously the claim that the church's first act must be to make a "preferential option for the poor" by looking at all existing proposals for change first of all in the light of what they do or do not do to help alleviate the massive poverty of the great majority of the human family. That, he reminds us, is where the Roman Catholic bishops in both South and North America came out. Not a bad place for the rest of us to enter in.

Robert McAfee Brown

Introduction

Why this book? Because I owe it. I owe it to those people who have been reading my articles for three decades. May I explain.

I love business. A glance at my journalistic resume would reveal that. I have been a New York associate editor and European bureau chief of *Forbes,* a *Financial World* Washington columnist, a *Financial Times* of London correspondent, a *Financial Planning* contributing editor, and a *Washington Business Journal* writer. My academic background is economics; my first book was on the U.S. economy. Though I love business, this book will strongly show that I don't like capitalism. And there is a difference, difficult to get at, but an essential difference that begins at a fork in the moral road.

For the past three decades, parallel to writing about big business and high finance, I have spent the years writing, too, on the poor, on the causes and effects of poverty, on people's struggles in the moral realm.

That writing has a major Catholic component, though for three exhilarating years early in the Reagan Administration I was also Washington correspondent for *The Progressive* (like my present employer and *Forbes,* great fun and a great challenge to write for).

The "Catholic" includes *The Catholic Star Herald* of Camden, N.J., *The Catholic Herald* of London, *The Tablet* of London, and, most valuably, *The National Catholic Reporter.* I left *Forbes* to become editor of *The National Catholic Reporter* in 1975 with the understanding that it would be for a minimum of three years, a maximum of ten.

I was there for five years as editor then returned to full-time writing, including for many of the publications listed above. By that time also I had written *The Decline of*

I

Capital (T.Y. Crowell, 1976), a book on the U.S. economy: where it was headed (down), and why (in brief, because the U.S. appetite for goods was out of control, because the U.S. was no longer its own self-sufficient supplier of its major raw materials, because U.S. goods could not compete globally except in aerospace and computers).

Four years later, I wrote *Reassessing* (Sheed & Ward, 1980). This was an attempt to address individual Christian conduct in an economically interrelated and interdependent world. It was done as a reflection and addressed to the first world Christian seeking an anchor point in the storm of affluence and materialism swamping America's own worthy verities. It was a new form for an old piety (in the best sense of that word), the rosary.

It is in *Reassessing* that the obligation to write this book is rooted. Here was the moral challenge I faced. Few people have had the opportunity to simultaneously work both sides of the economic canal, so to speak, as I was doing—writing on both capitalism and poverty-social issues. The time *had* to come when I answered the question, "Well, what do *you* think?" I had to be able to answer in the light of the Christian teaching I try to follow, coupled with my knowledge of the pragmatic business world that also is part of the kingdom. I had positioned myself with one foot on each side of the canal.

This book began more than a decade ago with two articles under the heading, "Christ as Economist," in *The National Catholic Reporter*. Through three drafts I have attempted to synthesize what I have been reporting and writing about in this country and from around the world for more than thirty years—as it applies to the Christian concerned with morality in economic life. In 1991, I crunched the 100,000 words of the third draft into eight columns, again for the *Reporter's* pages. Using those columns as the chapters, I then rebuilt the book into something less telegrammatic than a six hundred word column. This is the result.

After the "Christ as Economist" articles had appeared, I had three friends who particularly urged me on: the late theologian and Methodist historian, Dr. Albert Outler, the late editor-in-chief of Orbis, Philip Scharper, and the very much alive *Reporter* editor, Tom Fox.

Many people were generous in reading drafts, including my friend—and *Reporter* board chairman when I was president—John Caron, who built up his own multinational corporation and who finds very little to agree with in the chapters which follow. I also want to acknowledge the work of my chum, Spiritan Father Edward Kelly of Our Lady Queen of Peace Catholic community in Arlington, Virginia, on the discussion questions and the continuing inspiration of my other chum, and pastor, Spiritan Father James K. Healy.

Nonetheless, I take responsibility for what follows. It will dismay many of my financial journalism colleagues and some of my good friends in corporate management and investment circles. Yet it is the summary of what I truly believe, on reflection, about where capitalism starts to go wrong and about applying Christian teaching to the economic scenes of wealth and poverty with which I have become so familiar. This book is not based on collected wisdom, but collected experience. It is the work not of an intellectual, but of a journalist.

And it has had, as a continuing impetus, one incident I shall never be rid of. I had seen poverty in refugee camps in Somalia, in cities in India, in European and American slums (the latter during 1966-68 working for the War on Poverty in Newark, Trenton and Washington, D.C.). But I didn't have an answer to one question I was always asking

myself—and I've lived primarily in the United States
since 1958—and that question was: How poor is poor in
America?

In the mid-1980s, in the loblolly pine forests of Alberta, Alabama, about forty miles southwest of Selma, I
was given the answer. Alberta is little more than a cross-
roads, and where the roads cross was a trailer in which
two nuns ran a health clinic. I talked to them for quite a
while, and then, just as I was about to leave, I asked the
obvious question: How much do you charge?

"We charge two dollars," said the nurse practitioner,
"and the people are very good about paying. Most of them
pay one dollar down, and the rest off on time."

People so poor, they had to pay a dollar off on time.
That's how poor the poor are in America.

Two dollars where I live is a meager tip; teenagers
wouldn't bother to pry open the grid or scramble in mud
looking for eight quarters if they accidentally dropped
them in a drain. They'd shrug and walk away.

So, I had the answer to my question, "How poor is
poor in America?" And now I have to keep asking,
"Why?" This book is one answer.

Arthur Jones
Alexandria, Virginia
1992

Chapter One

Business is a combination of war and sport.
Andre Maurois

The Catholic Church is opposed to capitalism, which concentrates the property in the hands of the few, and to communism, which concentrates it in the name of collectivity.
Fulton J. Sheen

That which was death to Catholicism (the beginnings of modern institutions based on greed and pride) was actually the birth of capitalism.
Gilbert K. Chesterton

The human inadequacies of capitalism and the resulting domination of things over people are far from disappearing.
John Paul II
Centesimus Annus

"Capitalism" is a trick word. It has to be nailed down. Capitalism used to mean the creativity of business (entrepreneurship) combined with the benefits of competition (free enterprise, the market system) with the profits going to the entrepreneur and the investors. The classic definition of capitalism was "the private ownership of the means of production."

In the 1950s, in corporate America, most of those definitions fitted. Today, "capitalism" does not mean these attributes—though capitalists would like it to.

"Capitalism" as now used can best be understood as one word describing three states of economic activity: capitalism the good, capitalism the bad, and capitalism the ugly. Business, however, needs to retrieve its good name. So, while noting here that business can be seen as "capitalism the good," from now on "capitalism" will mean "capitalism the bad and the ugly."

Why?

Because capitalism the bad and the ugly is today's first world economic way of all flesh that brings plant closings, pollution and unrefundable third world debt. This capitalism encourages us in our existing selfishness; it blinds us into accepting a status quo that in fact sorely needs changing.

This is the capitalism that feeds off the good image of honest business decently run.

Bad and ugly capitalism, quite simply, is business corrupted. Why should Christians care? Two reasons: because capitalism—bad and ugly—creates injustice, certainly; but equally because its defenders want to root capitalism in the deep moral soil of scriptures and the Judeo-Christian heritage. But the capitalism described here is a pernicious weed to be uprooted, not a seedling to be nurtured. As the British writer John F.X. Harriott remarked, "more insidious than atheistic materialism is materialism with a Christian veneer."

This capitalism does not want competition or open markets—though business may. This capitalism wants monopoly, control and a risk-free environment.

To the open-minded Christian, good business (capitalism the good) is surely as creative and honorable a human pursuit as any other in the eyes of God. The business person, utilizing the best of a God-given talent, does create—can create—something wholesome. And this is analogous to the artist using God-given talent.

If these pursuits make money as a constitutive part of the pursuit, that's great. They must, to survive. Pope John Paul II recognizes that. But if the artist/business person knows in conscience that this activity is *solely* for the money—that is a form of self-corruption. And Jesus has something to say about talents wasted.

Though joined at the hip like Siamese-twin economic systems, capitalism and business are one unit with dual personalities: capitalism is one thing, business another.

Capitalism's stages, nailed down, look like this:

1. Business (capitalism the good): *Ignition*—the entrepreneurial stage that creates wealth where none existed by teaming together ideas, capital and human energy. *The beneficial*—the newly freed wealth creates jobs and income for the community. Business is every commercial enterprise honestly run, from corner store to major hotel to international corporation, in which the human element takes equal place to the need for the profits that ensure survival.

2. "Capitalism the bad": This is both a stage and the *process* of business being corrupted. It may create jobs for some and profits for others, but someone is going to suffer as profits are maximized.

3. "Capitalism the ugly": Business thoroughly corrupted; greed reigns supreme.

Capitalism's defenders imbue capitalism with moral sensibilities and sensitivities. Capitalist apologist Michael Novak, for example, contends that capitalism "operates neither outside the law nor outside morality. Capitalism is paired with a political system (republican self-government) and a moral-cultural system (largely Jewish, Christian and humanistic) both of which properly check and guide it."

Even the most cursory reading of the daily newspaper headlines or magazine stories during the past decade casts doubts on the contention that either the political system or the cultural system can or does check or guide capitalism. Rather, capitalism appears more likely to suborn the political system to its own ends while ignoring the moral-cultural system's proscriptions. Indeed, on the latter point, the neo-conservative writer Irving Kristol, in his book *Two Cheers for Capitalism*, found the moral-cultural system on which Novak is depending (and which Kristol describes as the nation's "accumulated moral capital") almost depleted.

A half century before Kristol, Peter Drucker, an American whose name became synonymous with U.S. managerial expertise, complained in *The End of Economic Man* that capitalism subordinates all other human progress to economic goals. Drucker contended that to achieve individual freedom and equality required "a new non-economic social concept." The writings from many Christian church bodies, including recent papal teachings and those of national Catholic bishops' conferences, all simmering in the pot tended by Christians seeking salvation, may yet provoke this "new non-economic social concept."

Indeed, to this end, many Christian churches in the 1980s and 1990s deepened their examination of economic life in the capitalistic world. In 1986, the U.S. Catholic bishops, after wide consultation with American Catholics and non-Catholics, issued their pastoral letter, *Economic Justice for All: Catholic Social Teaching and the U.S. Economy*. Catholic bishops' conferences in Australia and Canada have issued their own extremely strong critiques, and elsewhere, in the Philippines, for example, economic injustice is discussed in pastoral letters that also deal with other forms of oppression.

American religious bodies such as the United

Church of Christ ("Christian Faith and Economic Life"), the Lutherans ("Community Economic Development as Mission") and the Episcopalians ("Economic Justice and the Christian Conscience") have deeply involved themselves in the moral economic debate.

Evangelical Protestant Professor Richard J. Mouw has stated that "the Roman Catholic bishops are convinced that the gospel provides us with a solid case for the preferential option for the poor . . . and it is difficult to imagine how any Christian might set out to deny their point. The bishops are not alone in viewing present-day economics in terms of spiritual and moral crisis." Interestingly, Mouw's observation came in a book, which shows the interfaith interest in moral economics, *Prophetic Visions and Economic Realities: Protestants, Jews and Catholics Confront the Bishops' Letter on the Economy.*

All these examinations concentrate on two facts— that the Christian or Jew ought not to subdivide his or her life into two compartments, "God" and "world." Then, given that, these examinations explore how the believer might make sense of economic life.

Capitalism is not simply an economic system, however; it is also a state of mind, an attitude. And there has been an attitudinal shift in this century. *Forbes Magazine* provides one example of that shift. In 1917, when B.C. Forbes (Malcolm's father) started *Forbes*, above the editorial page he ran (and it continues to run) the legend: "With All Thy Getting, Get Understanding." B.C. Forbes implied that there is a moral component, a moral charge, to acquiring, to the acquisition of wealth.

Move forward seventy years. The German magazine group, Burda, strikes a deal to bring out its own *Forbes*-style magazine in Germany. Said Burda, in *Forbes'* pages: "The younger, business-oriented German readers, like their counterparts in the U.S., have developed different attitudes toward money and success than the generation before them. They subscribe wholeheartedly to the *Forbes'* philosophy: Get rich and enjoy it."

That's what capitalism has become.

Some attribute the depletion of the nation's "accumulated moral capital" to the decline of the WASP code, to the erosion of the Golden Rule Christian ethics of the White Anglo-Saxon Protestant ruling elite of the eighteenth and nineteenth century. Vestiges of that code did survive into the first half of this century to act as the "moral cultural system" checks to which Mr. Novak refers.

Finally, also by way of introduction, two other observations need to be made about capitalism: one, that capitalism cannot be blamed for all the world's ills, and next, that capitalism has provided us with at least one gift: the big picture.

The world's ills have several causes. The Christian Medical Mission, reporting to the World Council of Churches (the Geneva-based organization of world Protestant and Orthodox churches), stated that "the number one cause of disease in the world is poverty, the end result of oppression, exploitation and war." Economic injustice, economic inequality, are only one part—though a major part—of the problem, and of poverty. Pope John Paul II said as much in his writings when he has spoken also of the poverty when human and religious and economic freedoms are denied.

Capitalism's gift, the big picture, can be understood this way. Multinational corporate capitalism has given humanity a working model that shows how world-scale economics can function. Private enterprise unleashed in the pursuit of maximized profits has demonstrated that five billion people *might* be reached on a single day with a single product or service. Prior to modern capitalism, there was no model for a functioning and interdependent global economy.

Capitalism has not done what is needed, it has shown what is possible.

Capitalism, for profit, has laid the groundworks, the networks, the roadworks, the distribution systems, and provided the knowledge of how to manage immense large-scale organizations, the mass communications and global transportation systems, the technologies and packaging that could feed, clothe, doctor, educate and house the whole world from scratch—possibly within a decade.

A consortium of capitalist transnational corporations could probably do in ten years what a consortium of well-disposed national governments and global service agencies have failed to achieve in a half-century: redistribute the world's goods and services according to need and implement the required social development.

But capitalism will not do that.

Capitalism will not save the world, in that sense, because it has no motive for doing so. There is no buck to be made. All that capitalism can do—and at its best do brilliantly—is find new ways of making a buck. Capitalism, by its very nature, quickly conditions the world around it so it can extract for itself the maximum for the minimum. That is capitalism's sole goal, its unique purpose, and in the final analysis—measured against a yardstick of Christian values—it is a goal and a purpose insufficient and unworthy. What the world needs, of course, is a system that gives, not takes, the maximum for the minimum. But capitalism, left to itself, would go from cutting costs to cutting corners—for the end is never the common good, but the maximum profit. The end is not a common good for which capitalism could fashion a delivery system; the end is the maximized profit which alone would attract it to the venture.

In bad and ugly capitalism that end, the maximized profit, is frequently sufficient to justify the means. Capitalism tells the individual that "self-interest" and "success" are virtuous, that money and material worth are the measure of life. As the car bumper sticker reads: "I want mine and I want it NOW." Capitalism offers itself as an alternative value system and, like a religion, requires a conversion to its concepts.

The Christian has a very different starting point. The individual is called to selflessness, not self-interest; not called on to succeed, but to "do," whether that doing leads to earthly success or not. Economic organization, from the Christian perspective, begins with the fact that God gave creation for distribution among all people, and down the ages. Fair shares, and an eye to the future. Arranging this distribution equitably, with the poor in mind, is part of building the kingdom of God on earth. It is a key component of the good news.

However, as the late Atlanta Catholic Archbishop Paul Hallinan wrote, "the good news of salvation has not had a good press," and Christian critiques of capitalism rarely do, either, even when written by popes and bishops.

Chapter Two

I can see in principle no grounds for that low estimation of the creation of wealth which prevails in many Christian circles and which regards nursing as inherently more vocational than oil drilling.

Rev. Anthony Dyson
Canon of Windsor, England

The modern business economy has positive aspects. Its basis is human freedom exercised in the economic field, just as it is exercised in other fields.

John Paul II
Centesimus Annus

It is a socialist idea that making profits is a vice. I consider the real vice is making losses.
Winston Churchill

The church acknowledges the legitimate role of profit as an indication that a business is functioning well.

John Paul II

To examine capitalism-the-good (business) requires first asking: (a) How come Christianity involves itself with economics? (b) What price do Christians pay—why does the western capitalist media call Pope John Paul II a socialist when he examines capitalism?

Having taken a quick look at those answers, then we

can understand the actual value of the praise when pope
and bishops *do* heap compliments on good business people and good business practice. Obviously, Christianity is
involved in economic questions because values, morality,
are involved. This is what the church teaches: not just
fides, faith, but mores, conduct.

Economics is more than just one vital life-giving
arena. John Paul has said, "Work is the key to the whole
social question." Work is good if the worker is good and
conscientious, if the workplace and conditions are decent
and the work itself beneficial to society.

The opposite of this "good" is bad, sinful, and the
Catholic Church recognizes that we are capable not only
of "personal" sins, but of "social"—including the economic—sins. Indeed, in addition to the seven deadly sins
we've heard about, there exists in the Christian schema
"four sins which cry out to heaven for vengeance," and
two of those are economic sins: "oppression of the poor"
(Ex 2:23), and "defrauding laborers of their pay" (Jas 5:4).

Christians confronted by wrongdoing become indig-
nant; our Christian conscience should impel us to combat
that wrongdoing, to express moral outrage or take those
acts which require great moral courage. As this century
ends, we are learning more adequately that we must
move against economic wrongdoing and unjust economic
situations.

Christians have performed "economic acts" that required great moral courage in this and other centuries
and many continue—for example, those who live and
work with and for the poor, such as the Catholic Workers
or those in religious life dedicated to these goals. But as
this century, with its great emphasis on economic self, on
affluence and materialism, draws to an end, even people
attempting a simple lifestyle are courageous. Their act
requires them to be counter-cultural.

Living out Christian ideals as a business person equally can be counter-cultural. There is great demand in that situation for the conscientious Christian. After all, economic life determines who gets the treasures of creation, and which portion goes to whom.

In the first world, the only alternative moderator to market capitalism for this distribution of creation's gifts is the government—through laws and regulations.

So, persons dedicated to ensuring that their business remains profitable—in order to remain in business— and those in government who have a role in economic decision-making equally carry a moral charge and a moral burden.

But who teaches about the morality of this economic life?

Just before the pope produced his 1991 encyclical on capitalism, *Centesimus Annus, Boston Globe* columnist David Warsh wrote that "for every person who gets his or her economics from a textbook, another hundred or so people around the world get theirs from the Roman Catholic Church."

What we see in our lifetime is that Christianity is learning how to be a better teacher of economic morality. Yet we are also learning from Christianity's own origins that Jesus knew all about business and wealth, and so did his listeners.

The first "economic" people mentioned in Matthew are fishermen—they own their own boat. We meet salaried people, the centurion (Mt 8:5) and the "official," obviously comfortably off (Mt 18:24). The shepherd retrieves his sheep (Mt 12:11) not only because he loves them but because they are also his economic livelihood.

The gospels deal in a cash economy, the half-shekel for the temple (Mt 17:27), the moneychangers in the outer courtyard. The rich young man (Mt 19:22) does not need

to be explained, nor does Joseph of Arimathea (Mt 27:57).
Jesus' listeners knew what a rich man was, and what laborers were, toiling in the vineyard (Mt 20:12). The absentee landlord (Mt 21:33), familiar to West Virginians
living among strip mines and to tenants of slum landlords,
was known in Christ's time. Listeners understood sufficient economics to follow the worldly side of the man
investing in the pearl of great price (Mt 13:45); had they
not done so the parable would have made no sense to them.

The parable of the talents (Mt 25:14) is almost out of a
modern investment handbook: if no other more profitable
investment avenues were open, at least "you should have
deposited my money with the bankers and on my return I
would have recovered my capital with interest."

Those people of Jesus' day could taste and touch,
imagine and feel the satisfactions and comforts of material wealth just as we can.

Jesus understood what it was he was asking people to
forfeit. Today's Christian teachers equally understand
what it is they are asking us to forfeit as we are asked to
share creation's goods with the world's poor and save the
world's resources for future generations.

But our number one trouble is that we don't want to
relinquish our comforts and conveniences. Then, number
two, the capitalist system which brings us these comforts
does not want to be changed, either.

Next, the number three first world problem, one we
do not want to even face, is how wealthy we truly are.
And what has made us wealthy is the efficiency with
which our businesses, under global capitalism, have garnered this country's and the world's riches and markets
and fed them back to us.

How ironic then that, just as we personally finally
seem to be doing reasonably well, we are being drawn

into an economic reality where the inequality of it all, the injustice of it all, the injustice of the fact we are using up unfairly other people's portions, makes everything a moral debate for the many Christian churches and a moral charge on our consciences.

Where our western economic structure is concerned, belatedly, we are beginning to see what is involved. Post-World War II was a sort of mildly heroic stage of U.S. corporate business (and good capitalism.) The nation, still scared of and scarred by memories of the Great Depression, had not abandoned its sense of thrift. The economy was more or less in balance.

Organized labor ensured that the worker was heard through collective bargaining; corporations were reasonably responsible to their stockholders and customers, and President Eisenhower could say with a straight face: "Church by all means on Sunday—but what is the use of church if at the very center of life a man defrauds his neighbor and insults his God by poor craftsmanship."

Until a couple of decades ago, as far as most Christian teachers and preachers and practitioners were concerned, business (capitalism the good) functioned on the premise that an entrepreneur could make a fortune meeting the needs of the public. And, in its odd sort of way—the rich have to contend with God on God's terms not ours—the fortune didn't matter so much.

Even until a decade or so ago, most of us did not clearly see the costs of allowing the individual, or the corporation, or the industrial-financial-technology-rich first world to go fortune-hunting and fortune-making in this way.

Now we have no excuse. Now we know.

We know the consequences of our comforts, our cars, our consumption—six percent of us in the United States

consuming twenty-six percent of the world's annual resource production. Our capitalism has brought that to
us. So?

So, we pose the question to ourselves another way: If
capitalism is so bad, so ugly, how come eastern Europe
and the Soviet Union want it? The answer is: They don't.
They want business in its first two stages: the ignition
stage and the beneficial stage.

Desperately struggling former "iron curtain" nations,
eager for economic growth, nonetheless dissect this capitalism we have mindlessly supported. Czechoslovakia's
new president, Vaclav Havel, declared: "We want democratic principles from the west, but not all the materialistic values." Soviet president Mikhail Gorbachev in November 1989 pleaded against the export of capitalism to
the east, and called on the communist east and the capitalist west "to meet each other halfway." Gorbachev said
that when "accusations of 'exporting revolution' are replaced by calls for 'exporting capitalism' we have at hand
a dangerous manifestation of the old thinking."

What is needed instead, said Gorbachev, is the understanding that "the modern world does not consist of
two mutually exclusive civilizations but one common civilization in which human values and freedom of choice
have primacy." So, even those in desparate financial
straits, the new European democracies, could see—as
John Paul II so clearly sees—that capitalism is not an un-
alloyed blessing. Such a critical perspective sits hard with
the western press which frequently has called the pope a
"socialist" because of it.

In 1991, just as the pontiff was preparing his encyclical on capitalism, *Centesimus Annus*, to mark a century of
papal economic encyclicals, John Wyles wrote in the *Financial Times* of London, "The Vatican is nervous about
acquiring political labels, but John Paul II has long been

one of Europe's leading socialists. Indeed, the pinkish blush which the church's social teachings have acquired over the past century . . . has been given a deeper hue by [John Paul's] two social doctrine encyclicals, *Laborem exercens* (1981) and *Sollicitudo rei socialis* (1987)."

The U.S.-published *National Review* in 1991 ran a cover story featuring the pope's face and a headline which asked: "The Last Socialist?" Inside, John Gray wrote, "The pope's thought . . . endorses a baseless and misleading history of western capitalism and of the west's relations with developing nations." Gray continued, "While there are aspects of western capitalism that Catholic thought is bound to condemn, papal teaching goes astray insofar as it proposes radical alternatives to the system that has brought prosperity and liberty to western Europe, North America and, increasingly, the Far East."

In fact, the pope sees, as many Christians see, that the "prosperity" is illusory in all those places—the percentage of the poor is increasing rapidly. And there is not even the illusion of prosperity in the rest of the world. The pope, far from endorsing "a baseless and misleading history of western capitalism," was doing everything in his power to bring capitalism's true dimensions into focus for people everywhere.

This was the role, as economics teacher, that *Boston Globe* columnist Warsh referred to. Warsh wrote at that time, "The Polish pope has been privately accused of being anti-capitalist. This isn't surprising. The pope is a technically trained philosopher who lived most of his life in a Soviet-dominated Poland. But he is widely seen as having played a key role in the systematic dismantling of Soviet hegemony in eastern Europe during the 1980s. John Paul is no sissy when it comes to talking about the bad points of totalitarian communism."

What we shall face in this book, and in our lives as

counter-cultural Christians, is that some people cannot tolerate criticism of the bad points of capitalism.

Capitalists want the churches to stick to "saving souls" rather than stick their noses into economic issues. A *Wall Street Journal* (August 30, 1988) columnist reflected this mood perfectly when he wrote that "businessmen can't understand why clergymen attack the U.S. economic system when it delivers so much material abundance."

What Christian questioning is doing, of course, is delving into the *actual price* that the world, particularly the world's poor, pays for western material abundance.

All of this, nonetheless, does not condemn *business*. By the 1980s, in fact, with the moral economic examination well underway—and it could be said to have increased its momentum with the start of John Paul II's pontificate in 1978—the U.S. bishops did recognize the worth of honorable business people. (Those same bishops mildly damned capitalist excess though their boss does it it in bolder words).

In their 1986 pastoral letter on the U.S. economy, *Economic Justice for All,* the bishops praised "conscientious business people [who] seek new and more equitable ways to organize resources and the workplace. They face hard choices over expanding or retrenching, shifting investments, hiring or firing." (How tough this was the bishops themselves knew: they urged "full employment," but many were laying off workers in their own dioceses.)

Also in the mid-1980s, at the time the U.S. bishops were consulting widely with Americans prior to preparing the final draft of that economics pastoral letter, a group of conservative Catholics—including some of the bigger names on Wall Street and in U.S. corporate life—formed a parallel "commission." This group, the Lay Commission on Catholic Social Teaching and the U.S.

Economy, also held hearings and produced its own "lay letter."

That "lay letter' was pleased to quote Pope John Paul talking to Spanish workers in Barcelona in 1982. The pope then paid tribute to good capitalism, business:

"I greet and pay honor to you, the creators of jobs, employment, services and job training, all of you in this dear Spain who provide word and support for a great number of men and women workers. The pope expresses his esteem and gratitude to you for the high function which you perform in service to man and society.... Major errors were committed by entrepreneurs during the development of the industrial revolution ... but that is no reason for failing to give public recognition and praise to your dynamism, your spirit of initiative, your iron wills, your creative capacities and your ability to take risks."

The pro-capitalist "lay letter" then stated, "Willingly, we embrace this teaching."

There were and are many other major elements of the pope's economic justice teaching that the "lay commission" did not willingly embrace.

There is always more than one way to look at each economic situation. Here is an example.

The Australian historian, Jill Ker Conway, in *The Road from Coorain,* remarked that she "could not see what process but capitalism" was capable of turning Australia, populated by convicts shipped out from British prisons, into the "free society" it became.

Nonetheless, even she in time saw the other side of process, for she grew up on a sheep farm that failed. When she went to London she visited the offices of the finance company that acted as banker to many Australian sheep farmers.

Instead of skilled financiers she found "comfortable bureaucrats who throve on borrowing money at one rate and then lending it to gullible colonials at a three or four percent higher rate." With "Australia's predictable droughts," she wrote, it would only be a matter of time before many sheep farmers failed "and thus the land and finance company acquired its vast Australian holdings."

Capitalism's defenders would say that what the finance company was doing was simply straightforward banking. They would find nothing wrong with the means by which the company accumulated its "vast Australian holdings"—the company was simply taking the reward for having taken the risk. Others might argue that it was the farmers who were taking all the risks and the cynical financial bureaucrats knew it and encouraged it to happen.

Despite the fact that business is about money, there is nothing intrinsic in business that mitigates against moral behavior—not even in its ignition period, entrepreneurship. Management expert Drucker insists that entrepreneurship is a skill and can, like other disciplines, be learned. For many people business has its own excitements beyond money-making. Non-business people might find them dull, but a well-ordered business can be as pleasurable to witness as the workings of a well-crafted watch. A new invention, a new system, a new network made up of disparate networks, is creativity by any measure.

So, the good can be very good.

Nor is size always the governing factor on behavior: the local garage owner can be as unscrupulous as the most despicably behaved transnational corporation. But the very scale of corporate capitalism is what can wreak the havoc.

What we face is the need to ask: "How do we examine the motivation behind the economic pursuit?" *The Christian Century's* editors helped when they distinguished between "religious motivation" and "selfish motivation." They wrote that "religious motivation . . . is the inner sense that our needs are finally not as important as the needs of the larger community." Selfish motivation, they continued, "is the realization that each of us suffers when problems of poverty threaten to overwhelm either our society or our world. If society won't buy the first, it has to buy the second."

Good business accepts either the first or, through enlightened self-interest, the second. "Bad" and "ugly" capitalism allows neither motivation to govern its conduct.

Business (capitalism-the-good) has created and still creates for the world countless gains, from the benefits of electricity to the major advances in medicine, from the organizational knowledge required for the large scale, to the minute investigations that produce valuable new products. But it seems to be harder and harder to achieve this goodness.

The Reagan revolution of the 1980s accelerated the process already underway, one that made greed not merely acceptable, but preferable. As imprisoned Wall Street bond trader Ivan Boesky had explained it: "Anyone who tells you greed is a bad thing, I want to tell you it's not. And I think that in our system, everybody should be a little greedy. You shouldn't feel guilty."

Reagonomics and the Boesky attitude captured the enrichment-of-the-rich-at-any-cost attitude. Wall Street thefts, the S&L robberies, even prestigious bond trader Salomon Brothers' apparent ethicslessness, accelerated an already rapidly deteriorating moral economic standard. But these are merely examples for which we have recent names. Down through the ages, the economic sin has been a continuing one. Capitalism has enabled it to be systematized on a grand scale.

What we have to keep before us as we weigh capitalism-the-good in one hand and capitalism-the-bad in the other is that it is not "goodness" or a willingness to improve living standards that has made capitalism so huge. Rather, as Harvey Segal wrote in *Corporate Makeover*, the triumph of corporate capitalism "is a tribute to its functional superiority—it was clearly the most efficient way to organize and finance large undertakings" coupled (in this writer's words) with a zeal for maximized profits.

Business survival is geared to efficient marshaling of resources. That is not satisfactory to the Christian: the Christian obligation is to ensure that the marshaling is first of all just; that the treatment of the humans employed or served is decent; that the needs of the community are honored; that the corporate activity is moral in its usage of the scarce and ecologically fragile creation-granted world treasures, and truthful in its marketing and advertising claims and practices.

Even all this is merely the first step for Christians toward ensuring that everyone benefits from the creator's gifts. The Christian comes, as the pope comes, to teach and to change: "We are faced with serious problems of unequal distribution of the means of subsistence originally meant for everybody," said the pope, "and an unequal distribution of the benefits deriving" from those resources.

Business can aid in the just distribution of those benefits only if moral people are involved inside and outside the economic activity. Capitalism-the-bad and capitalism-the-ugly guarantee the unequal distribution.

That is the reason that those who have most to gain from capitalist pursuits do not like their economic world subjected to this Christian moral examination.

Chapter Three

Money is a stupid measure of achievement but unfortunately it is the only universal measure we have.

Charles Steinmetz

Profit is a regulator of the life of a business, but it is not the only one: other human and moral factors must also be considered which, in the long term, are at least equally important for the life of a business.

John Paul II
Centesimus Annus

We can't make a nation strong when it is held together by the rotten rope of self-interest. Too often we think of democracy only in terms of getting our rights.

Joseph R. Sizoo, DD

Always do right. This will gratify some people and astonish the rest.

Mark Twain

Capitalism-the-bad is both a stage and a process. And as we examine both the stage and the process we soon see why the Catholic Church and Christian teachers are involved in the issue. If capitalism at some point starts to shift from good to bad it is because people, actual individuals within the capitalist system, are shifting from doing good to doing wrong.

This chapter then deepens not only our knowledge of capitalism, but of the reasons behind Christianity's concerns with it.

Bad capitalism begins to emerge this way from good business. Captivated with, fascinated by its own needs—survival, efficiency, maximized profits—the corporation pays less attention to the "humanity" of its business. It is precisely at this point—as capitalism seeks to maximize profit—that the divergence from Christian precepts begins. This is the fork in the road as good, conscionable business diverges from the acceptable and the moral.

There is nothing wrong *at all* with sufficient profits to keep an enterprise in business and funding its future. But when business begins to seek the last ounce of profit, then the human factor, in some or all its dimensions (as employees, as neighbors, as consumers), is about to suffer. Bad capitalism has begun.

Christianity, as it deals with material wealth, has as its starting point a minimalist concept of "enough is sufficient." And even "enough" is too much when others are doing without. Excess, surplus, is not only unnecessary, it risks being wrong, it exposes its possessors to risking their salvation, their souls. To actively *seek* excess, surplus, simply to possess it, is most certainly wrong. Look at this from the perspective of the 1989 European Ecumenical Assembly in Basel, Switzerland as it laid out basic Christian and human attitudes toward the earth's wealth, our possessions:

> The life systems of our earth are irreplaceable; a thoughtless consumer approach to these systems will cause their destruction. I want to be aware that in buying, using and consuming air, water, earth, raw materials and energy, these elements are not available in endless quantities. There-

fore, I must learn to manage with less and to use
that which I need in a better way.

Contrast this with the attitudes of the capitalist intro-
duced below as he is on the verge of making hundreds of
millions of dollars in profit from a 1988 chemical industry
deal. The investment firm of Drexel Burnham Lambert
was, on behalf of itself and other investors, about to turn a
six million dollar investment into stock worth nearly five
hundred million dollars. "This is what is great about capitalism in America," said one of the investors, William J.
Gilliam, chairman of Rexene corporation.

So much for capitalists, but what of the chemical industry? A Dow Chemical Co. executive once told *Forbes*:
"At Dow we like chemicals. They are the only thing we
understand well. But chemicals to us are incidental to
making money for our stockholders."

Take a look at the environmental problems plaguing
the world. With the exception of our selfish fixation on
personal automobiles, fossil-fuel generated electricity
and the packaging and trash from our "convenience"
products, the bulk of all our other environmental problems can be traced back to the chemical industry.

Whenever an individual in any business turns a
blind eye to *anything* that might harm another, and that
is done toward maximizing that business' profits, that
single act is the sin which, in accumulation, creates in
capitalism the "sinful structure." (The "sinful structures"
are those to which John Paul II refers in his 1987 encyclical, *Sollicitudo rei socialis*.)

Again, what differentiates the good from the bad? It is
how the human element is regarded and handled as the
decisions are made. The drive for profits for their own
sake—profits beyond survival requirements—begins to
dehumanize; bad capitalism comes into being:

—Steel mill owners close down the mill and walk off without paying the pensions. International Harvester serves as one example.

—The factory knowingly continues to push unsafe practices on the worker: pick your packing plant.

—The quest for efficiency and productivity produces a sort of intermittent servitude—bordering, in some places, on a type of erratic slavery. Rawlings baseballs in Haiti; any sweatshop.

—The consumer is defrauded: adulterated baby foods; poisoned: any toxic waste site; deceived: Marlboro men with emphysema; diverted: coupons inside the packet distract from the price on the packet, a price based not on value but on what the market will bear (particularly so on supermarket shelves, for example, where two corporations control practically all the cereal products).

Bad capitalism is the transition to corporate abuse of worker, consumer, neighbor and the broader community; scarce resources are turned into today's profits without regard to the future; land, woods, air and water are polluted without regard to the human consequences.

These same problems quickly spill over globally. We quickly see, as we did with President George Bush's 1992 trip to Japan, that our government is essentially the representative of capitalism. He went as a salesman.

Let's just explore briefly that "bad capitalism" element as it might exist in first world governments. In Jalisco stadium, Mexico, John Paul condemned "unjust trade and financial practices." Capitalism will retort that trade is "satisfied buyer, satisfied seller." But it is not so when the first world deals with the third world.

What in fact exists is economic imperialism. In *Limits to Friendship: The U.S. and Mexico*, Robert A. Pastor and Jorge G. Castenada use phrases such as a relationship "between the dominant and the dominated" that take advantage of the inability of "weaker governments to resist the influence of more powerful ones."

So, this unfair advantage, by government or multinational corporation or financial agglomeration, this questing for wealth and dominance, is part of the equation in bad capitalism, too.

We can see it right inside the corporation, and measure it in yet a third way by looking at the pressures exerted within capitalist corporations that seduce or suborn the individual. (It must be said with equal force that these same pressures can exist in non-corporate environments, too: in the military, in the university, and, not infrequently, in the parish.)

A character in Loren Estelman's mystery novel *Silent Thunder* says, "You can't build a successful business and tend to family at the same time. One or other must suffer, and no one who chooses family ever had his picture on the cover of *Forbes*." Fictional but factual—we see individuals, this time the family, being relegated to second place behind ambition or "success."

It happens equally in real life. British businessman John Harvey-Jones was moving up rapidly in his multinational career. As he later wrote in the *Financial Times*, "I found the power and scale of the stage on which I now strutted difficult to adjust to. The lifestyle was a very far cry from the values that Betty [his wife] was building in our house. I began to grow apart from her, and from Gaby [our daughter], and our interests became more and more separate." The pressure to achieve within the capitalist system was taking over Harvey-Jones' life. Many middle-level and senior corporate executives could write the same story and merely change the names.

Then there was the executive who, not long ago, spoke of his far-sighted and humane corporation instituting a very liberal "paternity" leave. It positively encouraged fathers to take time off with their newborns. But this businessman was told by his boss: If you dare to take that paternity leave, the executive suite will hold it against you when promotion time comes around.

Some corporations have mixed reputations: Campbell Soup, until recent years, had a high reputation for quality, yet inspired a consumer boycott for its purchasing practices which were detrimental to migrant workers. Some corporations have reputations as good employers (Johnson and Johnson, Bell Labs and IBM come to mind); other corporations leave their employees bereft.

Corporate ethics, codes of behavior?

What about U.S. pharmaceutical corporations that dump in the third world drugs the FDA refuses to allow to be sold in the United States? Presumably their executives came from families with values, attended universities with honor codes, and work for corporations that give a nod to ethical standards. What about the Beech-Nut executives who sold adulterated baby food? They didn't suddenly emerge from ignorance into the corporate corridors. They, too, were exposed to some set of values that told them what was right and wrong. Yet they found the pressure inside the corporation such that they did what they did.

Even the advertising world probably has standards and code committees. But then, advertising has a way with images and words, and much of affluence's advertising in reality is quite a distance from Marcuse's remark: "My words must be good [not] only for moral reasons, but because society supposes that there are mutual obligations on the part of its members." Do the majority of advertising agencies, corporations, banking and financial services firms genuinely factor in those "mutual obligations"?

However, to return to an earlier point, it is not only

upwardly mobile *corporate* executives who are willing to sacrifice their families for success. Many a preacher, many a politician, many a political or social activist of left wing or right, many a college professor, many an actor, many a journalist, many a doctor has fallen for—or yielded to the pressure to accept—the combination of money, title or power that is called "success" in secular life.

Capitalism likes "success." Yet it revels in what can be a serious risk situation for the Christian. The Christian must not measure her or his Christian activities by the same yardstick that rules what "success" is in the outside world. For the Christian, the success is not in the *achieving*, not necessarily *in bringing something to completion* —such as eradicating poverty or disease. The Christian must be *doing*, whether she or he is likely to succeed or not.

Paulist Father Ellwood "Bud" Kieser, the man who produced the movie *Romero*, wondered why practicing Catholics caught up in business seemed to sometimes set aside their guiding principles. Then he read a UCLA study on just that topic. It showed that if you take people with high personal values and put them in a competitive situation where the stakes are high and the competition is close, those people tend to "jettison their values in order to win. Winning becomes the value," said Kieser. As for the individual, so for the corporation, and vice versa.

Yet this is not a burden that afflicts only practicing Christians. Bes Hussein, a decade after arriving from Pakistan as an immigrant, now owns five Washington, D.C. taxicab firms. He has acquired them, he admitted, at the cost of his identity and his religion. He admitted to *The Washington Post* that where his religion was concerned, "I wasn't exactly a mullah. I believed in certain religious and cultural values. What will I pass on to my kids? By our third generation they will be Muslims in name only. I thank God for all this success, but at times I feel it's really a curse."

Once a corporation or an individual accepts the secular notion of success, everything else becomes easier. It becomes quite simple to explain away one's vanities and arrogances, one's cutting corners, the little lies and dishonesties, then the big ones. Capitalism-the-bad can be seen in this loophole mentality, looking for a defense for the unethical, arguing that because something is not expressly forbidden it is therefore permitted.

"It's a loophole world, Puss," says thriller writer John D. MacDonald's hero, Travis McGee, "and there are a lot of clever animals who know how to reach through the loopholes and pick the pockets of the unsuspecting. There are a thousand legal acts that can be immoral, or amoral, acts." The sad thing is how many good people become trapped in the bad mess. Traveling by train in Europe one day I chatted with an executive from a Swiss transnational corporation. "Sometimes," he said, "I am not as good a Christian in my own home as I should be. So it isn't surprising that I'm not always as good a Christian at work as I should be." Yet, he continued, what made it less easy to be a Christian at work than in his home was the constant pressure of the highly competitive, efficiency worshiping, maximized profit-oriented corporation that demanded acts for the corporation's benefit that he was not totally comfortable with. He welcomed his forthcoming retirement as the event that would get him off the hook.

This executive had not sold his soul, but he had pawned it. Retirement was the only way he could redeem it.

Chapter Four

Man never fastened one end of a chain around the neck of his brother, that God did not fasten the other end around the oppressor.

Lamartine

Those whom fortune favors are admonished that they should tremble at the warnings of Jesus Christ . . . and St. Thomas Aquinas' words that man should not consider his material possessions as his own but common to all.

John Paul II
Centesimus Annus

Americans generally spend so much time on things that are urgent [that they] have none left to spend on those that are important.

Gustav Metzman

Ugly capitalism, what British Tory Prime Minister Edward Heath called "the unacceptable face of capitalism," is unacceptable on many fronts. Ugly capitalism produces "evil," it enshrines "greed," it is "exploitive."

Anthropologist Lionel Tiger described one facet of the evil in his 1987 book *The Manufacture of Evil* as the result of "huge, industrial arrangements of modern society [yielding] vast outcomes no one wanted, miserable outcomes nobody desires. In the industrial system, evil has become systematized, technologized, internationalized, multinationalized and, especially in times of war, rhapsodized."

"Greed," in the 1980s (the Reagan years), broke loose from the rough-and-ready and not-always-honored capitalist "honor (the expression is loosely used) code" into "sell, grabbit and run." Where capitalists couldn't sell, they stole—from the S&Ls, from the pension funds, from the Wall Street investor, from the government, from the public. It was what John Steinbeck called "piracy."

Much of this greed climate was wrapped in apparently acceptable economic techno-jargon, out of which came two phrases which, whatever their original intent and meaning, came to convey something else. The terms were "the trickle down theory" and "supply side." Both terms derive from the "constructive greed theory"—give the greedy what they want in terms of incentives (no taxes) and their pursuit of more money supposedly will benefit all.

Trickle Down: Essentially, the argument is that if the wealthy receive tax breaks, they will use this "extra" income to invest. That investment produces jobs, and jobs bring taxable income for the government to spend on social needs. It doesn't work. Look around. All that actually happened was that the rich got richer.

A New Zealand cardinal, Archbishop Thomas Williams, summed up the prevailing economic ideology of the 1980s and the early 1990s this way: "This pernicious 'trickle down' theory" means "no more than giving the rich more bread now so that the poor may have crumbs later."

Supply Side: Side with the wealthy and they'll supply the votes to elect trickle down supporters. Supply side offshoots included Reagan's wholesale deregulation—the corporate-governmental alliance's equivalent of the individual capitalist's "get rich and enjoy it" philosophy. The result for the nation was that financial capitalism sold off

U.S. industrialism for whatever price it could get, or closed it down, and took the money elsewhere—into leveraged buyouts or into the inflated-dollar purchases of cheap resources and factories around the world.

What is it, the curious might ask, that the capitalist wants? Not competition, but control and security. As Robert Lekachman said of PanAm's founder, Juan Trippe, "He was a firm believer in competition among his suppliers and monopoly for himself."

Bernard A. Weisberger wrote two decades ago: "The really big money is accumulated by shuffling paper, making phone calls and taking one's cut of the deal, rather than by actually operating hotels or car rental companies." It was no different in J.P. Morgan's day. As Morgan's biographer wrote: "Neither Morgan (nor his colleagues) could have told you what were the chief operating problems of the Southern Railway. . . . These bankers saw a railroad company as a group of men and a set of books; if the figures were satisfactory and were vouched for by reliable men, everything was all right."

Finally, where the capitalist cannot achieve monopoly, he will settle reluctantly for what is becoming the marked feature of our own economy, an oligopoly. That is where just two or three groups control the market: whether cereals, or toothpaste or transatlantic flights.

And as any customer knows, let that happen, and the prices skyrocket. Competition be damned.

Greed? In 1988, when *Financial World* magazine ran its annual list of top Wall Street earners (the most successful made more than $100 million personally that year), *FW*'s essay said: "Of the original 100 Wall Street tycoons who graced the pages of *Financial World* three years ago, six have been indicted or convicted of foul play. Only 6 percent you say?" There is a capitalism uglier than trickery and theft; it is the capitalism of brutality—a brutality frequently disguised from most first world audiences by distance and smart public relations campaigns.

John Ellis, in *The Social History of the Machine Gun,* quotes the harassed U.S. entrepreneur of the 1930s who remarked: "You can't run a mining company without a few tommy guns." During one strike John D. Rockefeller's police used machine guns. To recover, Rockefeller hired the first corporate public relations fix-it man, "Poison Ivy" Lee. The writer Robert Benchley later said, "Mr. Lee . . . has devoted his energies to proving, by insidious leaflets and gentle epistles, that the present capitalist system is really a branch of the Quaker Church, carrying on work begun by St. Francis of Assisi."

Machine guns yesterday, gas and truncheons today? In the late 1980s, an AFL-CIO official at a Washington, D.C. Wilson Center meeting on the U.S.-Mexican border maquiladora belt reported that when workers at the Mexican Electrolux assembly plant protested working conditions, company guards were ordered to gas them and Mexican police were brought in to physically subdue them.

Deplorable working conditions reached indecency depths in Haiti, where Rawlings was making its baseballs. Not only were wages $3 a day and the system fixed so that seasoned workers were fired to make way for a constant stream of lowest paid newcomers, there was little time off even to go to the toilets. But then, apart from a hole in the ground—there were no toilets.

At home and abroad, much of modern capitalism is reverting back to the worst excesses of its nineteenth century "Robber Baron capitalist" practices.

Details of these practices are generally absent from the U.S. media. The print and electronic major media do very little reporting on bad and ugly capitalism as a phenomenon even though individual cases of corporate abuse might be aired. When a scandal is so huge it cannot be ignored, such as the S&L crisis, it is usually that component of the capitalist system rather than the capitalist system as an entirety that is examined.

As we saw in the previous chapter, these larcenies and callous practices are not uncommon in the United States, pension funds are stolen, entire industries and huge corporate undertakings are allowed to collapse. Communities of thousands of families are wrecked as corporations make the unilateral decision to close down and move out—everything being laid at the most convenient altar of blame: foreign competition.

But if those companies were sold to the workers and local communities while they were still economically viable enterprises, the capitalists could still get out and the community still have a chance to survive.

Worker ownership and control does not guarantee that an entity will survive, but it would at least give it a fighting chance, as happened in the case of Weirton Steel and other similar worker-community ownership takeovers.

Peter Drucker, in *Concept of the Corporation*, rightly warned that the corporation "is a human institution and thus incapable of ultimate survival. To prevail for even as short a historical period as fifty years or a century is difficult for any man-made institution." (Drucker, in a merry aside, added that the Catholic Church, "with profound wisdom, points to its own survival over the ages as proof that it has been instituted not by man but by God.")

It is both the Catholic Church's sense of history and its worldview of human behavior and the human condition that makes the comments of popes and Catholic Christian teachers doubly telling when they focus on capitalism-the-ugly. There is unquestioned gravity to the charges when a pope makes them, as he did in Canada in 1984, charges that are twice repeated in this book:

"Poor people and poor nations—poor in different ways, not lacking food, but also deprived of freedom and other human rights—will sit in judgment on those people who take these goods away from them, amassing to themselves the imperial monopoly of economic and political supremacy at the expense of others."

At the very least, capitalism-the-ugly represents the worst elements of an economic way-of-all-flesh. Many first world critics of first world capitalist behavior do not anchor their criticism in the Christian sensibilities, but in common humanity. The economic oppression and dysfunctionalism we are witnessing, however, dramatizes more than a confrontation between two views of behavior. The extent of capitalism-the-ugly's activities, and the woeful paucity of a clamor against them, speak to the continuing and rapid secularization of society.

This "cultural shift of secularization," writes John Thornhill, S.M., in *Christian Mystery in the Secular Age*, "is one in which we all share. It touches the believer as well as the non-believer; it touches the man in the street as well as the philosopher and the academic."

To borrow Mississippi University Professor Gregory Schirmer's phrase, at the very least we are witnessing a broad "conflict between modern materialism and the need to believe in some kind of higher, transcendent reality." The driving force of this "modern materialism" is capitalism. Materialism is the new god, capitalists are its high priests, and the corporation is its temple. The analogy is not far-fetched.

Envision a temple and then remove all the high priests and replace them with new ones. Still a temple, right? Now let us borrow from Princeton Theological Seminary Professor Richard K. Fenn, in *The Secularization of*

Sin, to finish the picture: "What makes up the company is not individuals but positions. Empty the positions of their incumbents and put new ones in their places and it is the same company." If the individual wants to survive in a corporation that is dedicated to materialistic success, committed to maximized profits regardless of which corners must be cut, that individual has no choice; he or she will conform to what the corporation wants that position to do, or be ousted and summarily replaced. The bad or ugly corporation will continue toward its goal despite the crew changes.

We know what is going on when a pope or a church leader speaks out. Walter Schwarz wrote in *The Manchester Guardian* when *Centesimus Annus* was published: "Religion is about public, not just private, morality." So we see religion continuously gearing and regearing itself to grind into comprehensible nuggets and notions this materialism against which Christianity has pitted itself.

John Paul talks of the "temptation to base democracy on a moral relativism that reaches the point of refusing every certainty about human life and human dignity." The poor countries, he said, cannot be rescued by merely relying on capitalism's "market forces."

Capitalist materialism and Christianity each has a global reach—so when they confront each other, their confrontation, though played out in the first world, echoes and affects in major measure the rest of the globe. Indeed, religion is the advocate on behalf of the rest of the world. And as John Paul said in November 1991, the first world and the west cannot keep living "in an island of abundance surrounded by an ocean of suffering." Catholic teachers have been attempting to force the issue.

In *Prophetic Visions*, Robert Johnston writes that the U.S. Catholic bishops, for example, have much to teach people "about doing theology in the marketplace." The

authors of *The Emerging Order: God in the Age of Security*
reveal how even the pace of change works against those
who would combat capitalist materialism. "It used to be,"
they write, "that there were two distinct worlds, the
kingdom of God and the secular world. Now there are
three. The everyday world has itself become divided. Economic man and woman now live two separate lives, the
life of a producer and the life of a consumer. The consumer is cajoled, manipulated and encouraged to 'do it,'
to 'act,' and not to worry about the consequences."

The island of affluence the pope refers to is like a
coral atoll in which the coral is in fact millions of appliances. These purchased then junked appliances deprive
as well as serve. There are always negative consequences
to our purchases, to our economic behavior, to even
the slightest demonstration of our individual purchasing power.

Our wealth has been handed to us—we are wealthy
because of *where* we work (the first world) rather than
because of the actual work we do. Yet we still do not fully
accept this notion because in our materialistic culture we
have too many signals and messages, from our presidents
or our advertising slogans, from our schoolbooks or our
editorial columnists, telling us otherwise.

Christian and other religious teachers are attempting
to dissect this materialistic culture to detect and inform
precisely how it has changed or is changing us. That it has
changed, as F.X. Harriott wrote in 1989, is a certainty. The
tendency within the change that alarmed him most was
not the advance of "atheistic materialism," but the "more
insidious materialism with a Christian veneer."

Quite simply, neo-conservative writers, particularly
in the United States, are constantly attempting to present
what they call "democratic capitalism" as a human, ratio-

nal and just system which they see as worthy of the Judeo-Christian tradition's embrace.

The century of papal writing since Leo XIII's landmark encyclical *Rerum Novarum* in 1891, and culminating in John Paul II's centennial response to it, *Centesimus Annus*, rejects capitalism's benevolent view of itself and dismisses without qualification that it has a claim on the Judeo-Christian heritage.

Chapter Five

What does a democracy depend on? On the individual voter making an intelligent and rational choice for what he regards as his enlightened self-interest. What these [big advertising agencies] try to do is bypass the rational side and appeal to the deep unconscious forces below the surface. In a way they are making nonsense of democratic procedure.

Aldous Huxley

The loss of authentic meaning of life is a reality in western societies.

Pope John Paul II
Centesimus Annus

The starting point for dealing with economic morality is always the individual. And more often than not, the individual cannot quite see all that is going on. You have to be on the outside once in a while—like a theater critic on the aisle seat—watching *all* the performance and imagining the offstage elements of the scenario, in order to grasp the activity.

Sometimes we can come back from vacation—or particularly from another country or totally different environment—and see our situation, our country, our systems, with new eyes. Returning missionaries do this—it is one thing returned missionaries have in common, this crisp, unfiltered view of the first world society.

But most of us are a bit trapped and do not have the opportunity to take this more detached look. We in the

west, single or married, male or female, working or bat-
tling unemployment, are born into economic, political,
religious and cultural systems created centuries or mil-
lennia before we were born.

It is difficult for us to imagine *different* systems, *different* values, *different* ways of looking at things when
everything around us reinforces how we already look at
our lives. Religion, and certain cultural codes, are really
all we have that can provide us with different goals or
enable us to gain some detachment. Or sometimes a major change in our own circumstances forcefully yanks
loose the major bonds holding us to this status quo.

And yet there is in most of us, to borrow and bend
University of Mississippi professor Gregory A. Schirmer's
phrase, a continuing "conflict between modern materialism and the need to believe in some kind of higher transcendent reality." In the 1980s, California psychologist
Marsha Sinetar ran advertisements in local newspapers
asking: "Do you know someone who lives apart and likes
it?" She was looking for people who had found their own
way to detach themselves from the prevailing ethos by
living alone yet in a positive relationship with others,
who were supporting themselves financially yet looked
on their work as a devotional calling, no matter what it
was, who had a sense of "aesthetics, ethics and universal
order," and had designed their lives to be as simple and as
uncomplicated as possible.

Prompted by the replies she received, Sinetar wrote a
book, *Ordinary People as Monks and Mystics,* a remark-
able testament and inquiry and guidebook to pulling
back, pulling away, finding a means by which to take this
detached view. Even to think in this manner, of pulling
back, making do economically, is regarded as "counter-
cultural." It is, but then what we hear from Jesus, and
what the popes and bishops have written on our eco-

nomic lives, is asking us to be counter-cultural as part of our creative salvation.

While this book is about capitalism—and not just industrial and manufacturing capitalism, but financial capitalism such as banking and insurance, and service capitalism such as haircutting or counseling—we have to see that all our institutional systems have some things in common. The person working in a college or church organization, a government department or a not-for-profit-hospital, may see the same examples of generosity and meanness, caring and carelessness, kindness and pettiness, selflessness and ambition to be seen in the capitalistic world.

This is the human condition. What we are further asking, here, however, is what the capitalist system additionally adds to or detracts from this human condition. The prevailing capitalist ethos is affluence dependent on a crass materialism, a materialism promoted competitively with ambition as a virtue and wealth and possessions as the final worth.

Immediately, the wrong sense of worth, or what matters, has been created before our eyes. To utilize Oscar Wilde, the problem is not with the *average* American, but capitalist materialism's ideal American. And that ideal is created and sustained in all its emptiness through the worst side of advertising.

More than a century ago, in the 1880s, visiting British journalist George Steevens reported that "Americans are among the most demonstrative of all peoples on the earth. Everything must be brought to the surface, embodied in a visible, palpable form." Continued Steevens, "Materialistic in the sense of being avaricious, I do not think they are. But materialistic in the sense they must have all their ideas in material form, they unquestionably are."

But "materialistic in the sense of being avaricious,"

Americans have become. Advertising played into our
vanity. Yet at least in America there is a debate about it.
Some advertising people have scruples. The capitalist reaction to any such debate, of course, is: "Fix our ethics, by
all means, but leave our system alone." Capitalism does
not see itself as a *system* in need of reform; it believes
what it says about itself.

Alas, capitalism has become the dominant element
in the culture. Gary Edward of the Washington, D.C.-
based Ethics Resource Center even suggests that "the corporate community has replaced the church, the extended
family and even the community as the transmitter of values and ethics." If that is so, it puts capitalism at odds with
Catholicism, for, as John Paul II told young Poles at
Wzgorze Lecha in 1979: "Culture is, above all, the common good of the nation." Yet capitalism operates only in
its own interest.

Not every visitor in the nineteenth century would
have accepted Steevens benevolent view of U.S. materialism. Herbert Vaughn, a young English priest who eventually would become Cardinal Archbishop of Westminster,
was in America in the 1860s seeking funds for the Mill
Hill Missionaries. He observed: "If once turned to God
from materialism and mammon-worship, we are per-
suaded that the Americans would rank among the fore-
most Catholics of the world." Instead, a tyranny of value-
lessness has set in. It is the tyranny of a *system*.

We can see that dominating systems have much in
common. The following is from Pope Pius XI in 1939—
but where he said "communism," I have substituted
"capitalism."

> The capitalism of today, more emphatically than
> other similar movements in the past, conceals in
> itself a false messianic idea. A pseudo-ideal of

justice, of equality and fraternity in labor impregnates all its doctrines and activity with a deceptive mysticism which communicates a zealous and contagious enthusiasm to the multitudes, entrapped by delusive promises. This is especially true in an age like ours when unusual misery has resulted from unequal distribution of the goods of the world. The doctrine of modern capitalism, which is often concealed under the most seducive trappings, is in substance based on principles of materialism.

Does not our materialism offer a "false, messianic idea" leading us to view ourselves as the major objects of our devotions and energies? Is not advertising one form of "deceptive mysticism"? Is not the doctrine of modern capitalism "concealed under the most seductive trappings"?

Yet we are advised not to tamper with the capitalistic system which has built the affluent west and first world lest we bring everything crashing down. Eighty percent of the people on earth would scarcely notice. Another pope, Paul VI, when he was Archbishop Giovanni Battista Montini of Milan, said that people using "sophisticated formulae say: the economy is autonomous; it is queen; it should not be subject to moral scruples; we have to develop a free economy . . . controlled only by the built-in laws of opportunism and the play of the market."

But Archbishop Montini also argued: "The economy is a human fact which should obey human laws. Man is superior to the economy and the economy should be subordinated to man's use; not merely subjectively understood—because that would be egoism—but to the utility of the entire social world. In fact, the goods of this earth have to serve society, mankind, in toto."

Again and again we see the Christian teachers trying

to provide us with the distance from which to view our situation, and values with which to combat that in our economic situation which is unworthy, or bad or evil. The materialistic ethos, whether Marxist dialectical or capitalistic, decides our roles by telling us what we ought to be, defined by what we ought to believe and possess. Countering the capitalistic, materialistic culture is very, very difficult. If we begin with the ordinary individual, and look not at the poor, for a moment, but at the average American, what do we see the system producing?

A psychologist looking around metropolitan Washington, D.C. defined modern middle-class "stress" as the gap "between reality and expectations." When one young Washington couple decided to live on one income so that one parent could be home with their new child, they looked around and saw that "you've got neighborhoods where *all* the kids come home to an empty house. Big car, swimming pools, vacations—we can't do that," said the wife, "but it's a decision we've made together. It's not worth trying to 'keep up.' " Their attitude, certainly, is counter-cultural; it opposes the prevailing ethos.

What are we doing to ourselves, and offering to the new generations, but these preoccupations we have with a particular level of material possessions? Christian teaching is replete with warnings, and the major warning is the raising of a false god.

Is material progress or material possessions always bad? Of course not. John Steinbeck, down in the Sea of Cortez, looked at an Indian woman sitting in the gutter with a "repose beyond our achievement." But even these people, he wrote, "wish for our involvement in temporal and material things." The Indian, said Steinbeck, seems "rested, simple." But we should beware thinking the Indian's condition "superior to ours. The Indian, subject to constant hunger and cold, mourning a grandfather and set of uncles in Purgatory, pained by aching teeth and the sore eyes of malnutrition, may well envy us our luxury."

The capitalist ethos reassures us that we are worthy of envy. In fact capitalist materialism makes us make a virtue of ourselves. Because of this narcissistic ethos, we cannot see that we are merely mindless beneficiaries of an historical abundance, of an unchecked and profligate development of that abundance. In our vaunting vanity we truly believe we are entitled to all this by our daily work—when, in fact, most of our fortune comes from being in the right place at the right time in history.

We had an economic freedom unseen by any nation in all prior history. It was an economic freedom suborned by the materialism of the capitalist ethic.

Perhaps that is what most dismays John Paul in his numerous writings against capitalism and its selfishness. Our economic freedom that British journalist George Steevens admired a century ago became self-love—"a self-love," said the pope in Centesiums Annus, "carried to the point of contempt for God and neighbor, a self-love which leads to an unbridled affirmation of self-interest and refuses to be limited by any demand of justice." Such is our present day ethos.

The "ordinary people" who are "monks and mystics" in our time, even as they raise families or engage themselves in a full life, all see how life not merely changes, but improves, as they are able to hold material possessions at bay. Wrote one: "Having 'things' just interests me less and less. Conversation is more important than radio, television, movies." What a contrast to a world that occupies itself with gadgets and mindless entertainments supported by a system that cynically promotes personal ownership of every new fad the system itself creates!

We are drowning in the system's smothering self-promotion. And yet we have to free ourselves from it in order, as Christians, to help preach another way. In order to preach, we shall have to practice what we preach. That is a considerable challenge.

Yet what is it that we would preach? In former President Carter's 1991 words to church and political leaders and scholars in Atlanta, we must preach that "the greatest discrimination of all is the discrimination by the rich against the poor, and this troubles me very much because I am one of the rich, and so are you."

We are the wealthy—even though there are those who are wealthier than we are.

Chapter Six

What is condemned in class struggle is the idea that conflict is not restrained by ethical or juridical considerations or by respect for the dignity of others.

The church is well aware that in the course of history conflicts of interest between different social groups inevitably arise and that in the face of such conflicts Christians must often take a position, honestly and decisively.

It is right to speak of a struggle against an economic system if the latter is understood as a method of upholding the absolute predominance of capital, the possession of the means of production and of the land.

Pope John Paul II
Centesimus Annus

The global village is not a democracy. It is a plutarchy. That is, the world's member states are generally somewhere on the axis stretching between either plutocracies or military dictatorships. A plutarchy is government by the wealthy. We in the first world live in democratic plutarchies, plutocrat-dominated democracies, plutocracies.

Not every person of wealth actively participates in a plutocracy, though even the diffident and reticent appear when their money is threatened. (We are little different ourselves.)

First world plutocrats come in three types: (a) the

existing wealthy, (b) the get-it-while-you-can and any-way-you-can strivers (include here many corporate exec-utives, plutocracy's handmaidens, who share in the wealth by voting themselves large chunks of stock), and (c) the corporation itself.

Under U.S. law the corporation is treated like an indi-vidual. Given that, and the fact that the corporation's prime purpose is to create wealth, the corporation has the same drives, instincts and reactions as any other pluto-crat. What are those instincts and reactions? In short, there are three: self-preservation, self-enhancement, and "Hey, if I'm this rich I must be important!"

Economic self-interest is not limited to individuals and corrupt third world dictators, of course. National and regional governments can and do behave quite as self-ishly as the most selfish individual among us. One wing of capitalism makes much show of lauding what it calls "democratic capitalism," as if capitalism contributed to, or was healthily moderated by, the democracy.

What happens, of course, is quite the reverse: the de-mocracy is moderated by, on occasions controlled and di-rected by, capitalistic interests.

Capitalism itself has no ideological scruples. Where its business is concerned one does not necessarily find first world plutocrats and dictatorships, even Marxist dic-tatorships, at odds. There is usually a meeting of the minds, an accommodation, where money is to be made.

Most third world countries are dictatorships of vary-ing degrees of oppression or conformity. Who owns most third world economies? First world plutocrats.

First world governments frequently cast a similar shadow when their economic self-interest is at stake. In the case of the United States, for example (and the U.S. government is no more hypocritical in this regard than the British government), the government will tolerate behavior—such as human rights abuses—by oil-producing countries that it would publicly excoriate in countries to which it is ideologically opposed and with which it has no beneficial economic relationship.

China is an example of a country to which the U.S. is ideologically opposed yet whose human rights abuses are tolerated precisely because the U.S. wants a beneficial economic relationship.

When it comes to the third world's peccadilloes, occasionally even capitalists explode over bare-faced corruption. As the head of Germany's Commerzbank told a World Bank meeting in the 1980s: "I have not worked sixty hours a week for forty years so that some Argentinian army officer can siphon off aid money into a Swiss bank." (There is a less amusing side to all this. Impoverished by the easy loan money lopped onto them by first world banks and governments in the 1970s, the third world nations are now submerged in worsening poverty as high interest rates transfer the south's wealth to the north. In the late 1980s, a Latin American army captain was jailed for three years for robbing a bank as a protest against frozen military pay, the purchasing power of which had slid back to 1960s levels.)

Third world corruption is omnipresent. The Cameroons delegate told the 1990 World Council of Churches meeting in Seoul, Korea, that "the absence of democratic political machinery" means there is "no forum in most African countries where people can criticize leaders who steal the money and bank it in Swiss accounts."

Of course, people steal the money in first world countries, too. But the greater point is that in the democracies the plutarchs and their system frequently are able to "bend" or "buy" their governments. This results in what

Pope John Paul II condemns—the government "favoring one portion of the citizenship, namely the rich and prosperous."

Such bending of the government in the favor of capitalist wealth is an act against the common good, a social sin. Capitalism and the plutarchs avoid much of the censure they deserve because the bending takes place within the political system which seems to make it less objectionable. But the political system itself is a creature now of the plutarchs, therefore, capitalism.

In the United States, the Republican and Democratic parties, each in different measure, are plutocratic parties representing money.

One particularly vicious example of this is how the usury laws were abolished in the various states. Usury is the charging of unconscionable rates of interest on loans. With both political parties doing the abolishing, credit card companies, for example, can now charge eighteen to twenty percent on loans. That is usury.

Usury was condemned from the times of the earliest Old Testament teaching. Nehemiah 5:10 states: "Let us put an end to all this usury." The outright condemnation of charging interest on loans was modified during the reformation and post-reformation periods by both Protestant and Catholic leaders as it became apparent that "just" interest could be charged—but "just" did not mean charging whatever you could get away with.

In essence, "just" interest meant charging sufficient interest to make up for the money you would have forfeited by loaning the money to someone else. "Acceptable" interest was never conceived as charging whatever you could get away with.

When commercial interest rates and global interest rates oscillate between seven and twelve percent, credit card companies and department store charge accounts and the like cannot plead for eighteen and twenty-two percent interest rates on the grounds they are forfeiting those high levels of income by loaning to the hapless consumer.

Blinded by the snowstorm of materialistic advertising and pressures to buy, the consumer, with no firm foundation against materialistic affluence, is swept along.

One problem for today's first world generations is that they are uncertain: no one seems to educate them or to explain to them precisely what is unconscionable, or economically unacceptable.

Many churches and synagogue leaders do attempt this teaching role, as do many groups, but their criticisms are frequently drowned by the hype and advertising that promotes the commercial capitalistic cause.

For example, briefly in 1991 there was an attempt, by both the president and congress, to "cap" or to set a limit on the interest rates that credit card companies could charge. The speed with which divergent groups in the financial services industry organized their protest and demolished this capping attempt is a case study of the power-lobby of the plutocracy.

Unprotected, and unaware, are people who do not realize the speed with which the interest overwhelms them or impoverishes them. In a plutocracy, no one— again with the few exceptions already mentioned— is preaching thrift, recommending buying "used" and "second-hand" (as a matter of policy, not just out of necessity) or doing without in order to survive economically and as modest steps against future hard times.

What is preached by the governmental representatives of so-called "democratic capitalism" is that by following the present first world path, "things" will get better.

Not so.

The most that is happening is the periodic upward "blip" on a generally downward—for the U.S. and most of Europe—economic slippery slope. For the U.S. that slope started in 1965 when the country no longer had sufficient domestic raw materials to meet all its domestic demand and had to start scouring the globe to lock-up everyone else's.

In 1926, the United States was totally self-sufficient in everything except coffee and chrome. It was a self-contained island of indisputable wealth of such abundance that the world had never seen its like, nor had any nation of such size ever become so wealthy. So wealthy, but so briefly wealthy, for the resources were wasted, the future ignored.

To break through today's smothering onslaught of capitalist materialism to illustrate, to warn, to educate is an *almost* impossible task for moral leaders. Religious leaders, of course, are not expected to be deterred by the near-impossible.

In the secular field, possibly only the environmental movement at present has the potential to capture the public imagination and thereby educate the public in some aspects of what is happening economically. Otherwise, as has already been said, the political system is suborned and goes along.

So there are those churches which are alert to preaching economic morality more or less on their own, taking a stand but standing naked to their enemies as counter-cultural. Their enemies are the entire economic culture and its mighty publicity and marketing forces.

These capitalistic forces blanket the printed page, the airwaves, the entertainment media, and have created an entire values system which promotes exactly the opposite message. The sole goal is to make people part with what money they have *now* or with what credit they have *now* to satisfy themselves immediately, but in fact in order that the capitalist class further enrich itself *now*.

But why would members of the capitalist class go along with such a system. Surely they are individuals of conscience, too? Alas, plutocrats—capitalists and the executive class—are those people who "belong" to their money. It does not belong to them; they belong to it. The plutarchs' money *makes* them do things to preserve it and enhance it.

If the credit card interest rate "cap" reaction was an example of what the plutocrats will do as a group when its interests are threatened, then the 1980s and 1990s were filled with examples of the venality individuals will engage in to hold on to or make wealth achievable within this piratical system—S&L officers, the Keating Five, Milken, Maxwell, Boesky, dozens and dozens of knowns, lesser knowns and unknowns.

A plutocrat is someone who worships wealth. What money makes plutocrats do is commit social sins. The worship of personal wealth is the enemy of the poor.

But here's the rub for us, as American Christians. All of us in the first world, not on the scale of the plutocrats necessarily, but equally seriously if our comfort or convenience is threatened, can be encompassed within this "enemy of the poor" syndrome unless we are personally and deliberately standing against the selfish materialism which makes bad conditions for the poor worse.

In the non-capitalist, feudal or militaristic society— as in the modern corrupt dictatorship—there are additional powers wielded to make *a combination of powers* the enemy of the poor.

Contained, too, within this plutocratic sin, making it easier to commit, is first world cultural arrogance, a disdain for, ignorance of and a misreading of other peoples' cultures. This sin, Wilfred Cantwell Smith calls "the fundamental flaw of western civilization."

All right, so capitalism is the tool of the plutarchs. But it is more. In a sense, it is their private club. As *Financial World* stated:

> Call it a club. Call it a *banque d'affaires*. Or call it a holding company. The fact is that much of the world's business outside the United States is conducted through informal networks of industrialists, bankers and financiers who typically own stock in each other. Some steer business to other members of the group. Others do not. But all protect their members from the threat of hostile takeover. And most will protect their members from the threat of bankruptcy.

These are the powerful men who make presidents and break down the common good—precisely because it is common, not particular.

Plutarchs, capitalists, the corporate executive class, pit themselves directly against national social policies that would protect the consumer, ensure worker safety or help the poor or needy.

Two books reviews neatly capture this. Robert Sherrill, author of *The Oil Follies of 1970–1980: How the Petroleum Industry Stole the Show and Much More Besides*, later reviewed David Vogel's *Fluctuating Fortunes: The Political Power of Business in America*." Sherrill wrote of this "power business" and its common aims in attempting to manipulate government and national life toward its interests: "In the late 1960s and early 1970s [power business] tried but failed to stop enactment of laws promoting drug safety, honest labeling, clean meat in the market, truth in lending, occupational safety, cleaner air, cleaner water, and to stop the establishment of agencies to enforce those laws. To the businessmen that was a dark age, producing 'a series of setbacks without parallel in the postwar period.' "

Ronald Reagan, the plutarchs' president, banished that Dark Age, as John Kenneth Galbraith recounts. Galbraith, reviewing Haynes Johnson's *Sleepwalking Through History: America in the Reagan Years*, speaks of "the brilliant foresight and initiative that caused rich Los Angeles operatives to plan and support [Reagan's] tenure first in Sacramento and then in Washington, an exercise that paid off handsomely in a lovely experience at the inauguration made evident by stretch limousines for all; in later access; in political position for some; and in lower taxes for all."

Members of the clubs, whether Reagan's "kitchen" cabal or a French *banque d'affaires*, are admitted only if they are wealthy, appear wealthy, or do what the wealthy do and admire.

Many people—even executives—working within the good, bad and ugly capitalist enterprises, are caught up in the system but are not contenders for membership. As the Boston lawyer Frank complains in Richard C. Smith's, *A Secret Singing*, "they call us money-grubbing parasites, but that's not fair. We're just members of the salaried servant class. Overpaid and overworked." (There is a double irony in this comment. As the U.S. moves from an industrial manufacturing base to a service-industry base, the white collar class indeed is becoming as exploited, as overworked, as security-less as the blue collar workers of two and three and four generations earlier.)

And plutocracy becomes more than a club; it becomes a class system unto itself. As a class, capitalists, bankers, top corporate executives and investors, from

choice and circumstance, will usually have more in common with one another (regardless of their nationality)
than they do with the other classes within their own
nation.

Here is one result of that. Capitalism, to further enhance the plutarchs' wealth and to remain in business as
an enterprise (and make more money doing so) exports
jobs to a third world country. By default, third world economic conditions (joblessness, an eroding tax base, therefore declining educational and other social standards) are
imported. That is why we can now talk of "the third
world inside our first world borders," and we see it in our
cities and rust-belts and along our southern border.

All third worlds are poor, undernourished, ill-
housed, ill-educated and beyond the health-care system.
Ours is no exception. Third worlds also are cut off from
the advantages modern first world technology creates, yet
this technology provides much of the plutarchy's new
wealth and is the current hallmark of the first world
plutocracies.

In the United States, our domestic third world also is
cut off, therefore, from what has always been America's
major socio-political safety valve: a chance at upward mo-
bility. In the U.S., class divisions are hardening along with
the nation's economic arteries. The middle class is
shrinking.

The census and other studies show the United States
experiencing the continued enriching of the rich, and the
further impoverishment of the poor.

In *Centesimus Annus*, Pope John Paul defines "the
preferential option for the poor" as "a special form of primacy in the exercise of Christian charity."

In capitalism, under plutarchs, there is no preferential option for the poor, no special form of primacy for the

working poor (nor even, these days, for most of the middle class).

What, then, might we face? A class war along economic lines fought out politically and in the streets? The plutarchs' and corrupt dictators' answer to economic class warfare is, of course, the national security state. The common person's answer would be a democracy that includes economic democracy.

Yet to transform the plutarchy would require making the democracy truly responsive to rule from below, though in a plutarch-dominated democracy the chances of that seem slim. Catholic teaching does not like to talk about class enmity. And yet, as the quotations above from John Paul indicate, when conditions divide the classes, he is very aware of the necessity for the Christian to take sides—and which side they must take.

Chapter Seven

*Economic freedom is only one element of human
freedom. When it becomes autonomous, when
man is seen more as a producer or consumer of
goods than as a subject who produces and con-
sumes in order to live, then economic freedom
loses its necessary relationship to the human person and ends up by alienating and oppressing.*

John Paul II
Centesimus Annus

Time now, at the three-quarter stage, to step back
and review. Essentially, we have been looking at what is
bad in an amoral or immoral economy. Shortly, we will
look at what Christian teachers believe is good in a moral
economy.

How far have we come?

The cumulative charge to this point is that, measured
against Christian precepts, first world capitalist activity
(first world market capitalism, bad and ugly capitalism,
capitalistic materialism) is (a) detrimental to the common
good, (b) injurious to the planet, (c) but, worst of all, it
promotes a false god, materialism, in the form of personal
affluence and social "success."

The four major worries that arise for the Christian
are (1) that the quest for personal affluence contradicts
what God expects us to do with creation, (2) as we lopsidedly share out the world's wealth, we take essentials from
the poor by demanding non-necessities for ourselves, (3)
the ethos of capitalist materialism is smothering the
voices of individuals, families and major Christian religions alike that oppose this materialistic ethos, its values

and goals, and (4) there is an insidious attempt by capitalism's apologists to attribute Christian, or Judeo-Christian, values to this capitalistic materialism.

All this adds up to the present generations laboring under a tremendous burden of obligation to the future (and one not merely limited to moral economics, but the moral order generally).

We begin to see that unless people of faith, along with the humanists—and, to an extent we have not yet realized, the environmental movement—can make their case publicly and continually for people-and-creation-centered economic justice, the rising generations will be trapped in ignorance. When these current generations pass, succeeding generations (to borrow papal biographer William E. "Lilies of the Field" Barrett's thought) will rise no higher than their sources of information.

At one time, the school system and governmental behavior could be regarded as moral "sources of information," additional avenues along which precepts of morality could be channeled to succeeding generations. No longer, at least not on a grand scale.

Schoolteachers can barely control their students. The government is now the instrument of capitalism. As the United Church of Christ stated in its economic justice writings, corporate capitalism is now so powerful it steers the national economy and demands that the government intervene to promote multinational capitalism's interests.

School and government cannot be relied on to pass on or even bolster what's left of society's moral tone. We have entered the amoral night that succeeded what Richard John Neuhaus called "the dusk of the old-line Protestant establishment in American culture."

The "moral value" sources of information are being controlled by, or they originate primarily in, capitalistic materialism itself through its all-pervading ethos—and this will consolidate further unless the churches both preach and act, unless Christians reach out and live out economic justice by example.

Tough stuff.

Unless Christians continually find ways to witness counter-culturally within capitalistic materialism, the secularization of society gains greater momentum. The good people of the present generations cannot undertake this witness alone; we all need our moral compasses constantly trimmed and checked to make sure we're on course. That is why these papal and episcopal and individual Christian statements, thoughts permamently placed on paper and distributed as challenge and teaching, are so important.

One question posed earlier has to be faced again: Is this capitalism really as bad as all that? And if so, what are the moral components of building an economic system that is also moral?

Thirty years ago, when the worry did not appear so great, one of America's best-known writers on capitalism, Robert Heilbroner, stated, "I think it fair to say that capitalism as an idea has never garnered much enthusiasm. The acquisitive behavior on which it is perforce based has suffered all through history from the moral ambivalence in which it is held: all efforts to raise money-making to the level of a positive virtue have failed."

But in the decades since then we have seen a concerted effort to raise "money-making to the level of a positive virtue" that nearly succeeded. Indeed, had it not been for the rich-is-better Reagan-Bush-induced deficit-building recession, making money-making virtuous might have triumphed.

It is only the effects of periodic recessions that have most people suddenly examining their economy, not a sudden burst of moral inquiry. The Catholic bishops, for example, examined the economy when most Americans were experiencing Reagan-year good times bought by borrowing against the future through deficits.

But what about capitalism's defenders? What, by contrast, in the past fifteen years, have the neoconservative capitalists and the capitalist apologists been attempting to do? H. Assman, writing in the *Ecumenical Review* on the " 'Warm God' of the Global Market," lists among theological criticisms of capitalism's "economic rationality" that capitalism asks for submission to its spirit, and that spirit "purifies its own sins." To its proponents, "the global market is a messianic age of promises"; to its critics, in late 1980s and early 1990s, we entered capitalism's "charismatic age."

Further, as Assman sees it, to meet the Christian precept that creation's goods are for all, capitalism replies that the market will see to that. Assman concludes that the only universal base for economic justice is an ecumenical one based on the logic of the world's poor.

The popes—and in the Christian world they are not alone—argue the same premise as they seek alternatives to capitalism-on-the-capitalist's terms. Capitalism, John Paul II notes, "seeks to defeat Marxism on the level of pure materialism by showing how a free-market society can achieve a greater satisfaction of material human needs while equally excluding spiritual values."

John Paul would have no objections to "a society of free work, of enterprise and of participation. Such a society is not directed against the market," he writes. Yet he does demand "that the market be appropriately controlled by the forces of society and by the state" to "guarantee that the basic needs of the whole of society are satisfied." To state the obvious, when capitalism or the plutarchs control the democracy, "the basic needs of the whole society" are not, in fact, met.

But what are some economic building blocks that Christian teachers believe will help meet the needs of the whole society, regional and global?

In Spain's Basque region notably, and elsewhere, too, worker-owned-and-controlled enterprises are one first world starting point. In Australia, the Catholic bishops argued for more just tax policies, particularly in taxing inherited wealth. One U.S. corporate leader, William C. Norris (who attempted his own corporate responses to major social and economic problems) praised several key points in the U.S. Catholic bishops' 1986 economic letter.

The Philippines' Catholic bishops in 1990 argued that Pope Paul VI's theme, economic and social development, "to be authentic and integral, 'must promote the good of every person and of the whole person.' " They want dismantled the structures that favor the few, and the taxation system "that lies too heavily on those who have less."

All of this is beginning to sound very familiar to first world nations with third worlds inside their borders. On the first point, worker ownership, John Paul in *Centesimus Annus* praises the Christian contribution to "establishing producers', consumers' and credit cooperatives." There, he espouses what some people regard as a form of "people's capitalism"; yet John Paul equally firmly states that "the church has no models to present; models that are real and truly effective can only arise within the framework of different historical situations . . . for such a task the church offers her social teaching."

The best example of the modern cooperative movement arising from its historical situation is the Mondragon movement in northern Spain's Basque region. Founded just after the Spanish civil war by a Catholic priest, Father José María Arizmendiarrieta, Mondragon by 1987 was an association of one hundred and seventy-two worker-owned and controlled cooperatives that employs more than twenty thousand people, grosses two hundred million dollars in sales, stays abreast of the latest research, and owns the fastest growing bank in Spain—with two hundred and twenty million-plus in assets and one hundred and fifty-five branches.

Mondragon embraces ninety-four industrial cooperatives that manufacture everything from machine tools to refrigerators to auto parts; nine agribusinesses from cattle raising to forestry; seventeen housing cooperatives and forty-four educational facilities; a supermarket chain with two hundred and twenty-five outlets, plus research and development and technical assistance centers. During the 1981–1986 recession not one job was lost—workers took home eighty percent of their previous pay, worked longer hours, but were doing it for themselves, their community and their fellow workers.

At every level, through plant and regional councils, the worker participates in management, training and disciplinary decision-making. The Mondragon system incorporates some of the most advanced conciliation and worker participation programs yet devised. It *lives* Catholic social teaching.

So what is this Catholic social teaching already aware of? That when the workers own the factories and hire the managers, the factories don't flee. That when *all* of the community controls the resources it owns, those resources are treated with care. That when the poor third world nation with "commodities" can fairly trade in the open market, its people's lives improve. That when aid and commercial loans to third world countries are made only on low, fixed interest rate terms, there is a chance the money can be used for development and eventually repaid.

But in the west and around the world the economic system under capitalism is that the workers do not own the factories (investors do); communities do not control their resources (absentee landlords do); there is no fair market for commodities (the first world, often through International Monetary Fund and other quasi-governmental activities, controls the markets by way of currency exchange rates; thus there are overpriced first world manufactured goods and underpriced third world commodities).

And there is little chance, with today's overwhelming third world debt, that serious amounts of money can ever be borrowed for development unless existing debts are forgiven. No wonder, then, that John Paul II, in *Centesimus Annus*, can compare the "terrible conditions" of nineteenth century industrial capitalism—as depicted in Leo XIII's 1891 encyclical *Rerum Novarum*—to today's third world. Where is the Christian to look for strategies for change? Well, given that the pope has established study groups concerning family, he ought to give impetus to establishing similar study centers that could produce the substantive examples that his own economic teaching tantalizingly conjures up.

As Gregory Baum wrote in the Canadian context: "The ethical critique of capitalism emanating from these church offices leaves the great majority of Canadian Christians cold." The same can be said in the United States, Europe, the Philippines and Australia.

But what Baum goes on to say also holds true, that "a significant minority in these churches" *does* support the Christian critique by churches, popes and bishops.

But this significant minority in turn needs support from the church organizations in order to pursue and produce the hard examples that will witness economic justice to the world. For the fact is that to the Christian plunging into the economic problems of society, evidence of needed change is plentiful. It is the *means* for change that prove elusive—for there is no shortage of exhortation to change. Here is where popes and bishops grow particularly timid. They do not become living examples of the economic risk-taking and reordering they call for. Programs, yes. But not lived lives—not the church institutions "gearing down." The U.S. Catholics have the Campaign for Human Development, excellent provider of seed money community-based economic self-help projects. Its ten million dollar annual budget represents one Sunday's second collection. That is charity, not commitment.

The Episcopal House of Bishops, as with the ruling bodies of many Christian churches, has established "a ministry of community investment and economic justice directed to community controlled economic development programs: housing cooperatives, worker-owned developments, credit unions." Again, more excellent programs.

But there is practically no connection between the urgency behind these programs and the urging-by-example of how, say, practicing Catholics or Episcopalians, laity, priests, bishops, have to alter their lives, consumption patterns and financial priorities.

Fortunately, and increasingly so, there is something gnawing at the consciences or many Christians and their organizations which simply will not let the matter rest. By way of example, and one that can be replicated in documents from other churches, in 1986 the American Lutheran Church issued a study paper for its congregations and agencies on "Community Economic Development as Mission." It argued that "mission" is the "work God calls us to in this world" and that the churches, just as they pioneered schools, health services, food and agricultural programs, now must pioneer new economic programs. This is prophecy by example, of thinking globally and acting locally.

In the Evangelical Lutheran Church of America example, the paper called for debt-free local churches to borrow against their property to make capital available for community development programs (few Catholic bishops would like *that* approach), and asked that some of the church's own investment funds also be a source of capital. As the paper stated:

> It is obvious that church alone cannot meet even a small fraction of the capital needs of poor communities. But churches *are* in a position to provide an increased amount of capital on loan. What is needed . . . is to see that working to support self-sufficiency among poor people becomes a part of the church's mission.

We need to be able to "see" it.

So, for example, at its organizational level, the Vatican should at least have a "think tank" on moral economics to rival its studies on, say, science, interfaith concerns, or sexual behavior. But the pope and bishops, the Vatican bureaucracy and the diocesan curias, also should be seen as living examples of what is being preached.

In that way, and possibly only in that way, is the laity in its entirety seriously challenged to do what Pope John Paul II urged more than a decade ago, to give not just of our affluence, but of our substance.

What is being demanded of us is a way of thinking alien to how we—in our affluence—have gone about things. As James E. Hug, S. J. wrote in a Center of Concern "Scripture Sharing" on the Catholic bishops' economic letter:

> *All* of our economic decisions, from the smallest everyday purchases to the most complex na-

tional policies, are supported and guided by our
unconscious assumptions about life and our
hope for the future. It is important, therefore, to
reflect prayerfully on the tendencies of our culture—its strengths and its temptations. How are
we Christians, chosen by God and brought lov-
ingly through the waters of baptism, to respond?

And how are we as church, and as churches ecumeni-
cally united, to respond? The starting points are that the
poor come first and profit comes second.

This applies as surely globally as it does locally. In
1989, the vice president of the Vatican Justice and Peace
Commission said in Australia: "Profit is not bad in itself; it
should not be made absolute. If it is made absolute, it
becomes a 'sin'; indeed, 'a structure of sin' because it sub-
verts the true order of things, natural and supernatural,
and simply ignores the neighbor, near or far away."

The global responsibility of Christians, the delegate
continued, is "to introduce morals, ethics, Christian justice and love into the tight economic, social, political fab-
ric of this world. We do not want to limit such a 'global'
dimension to international bankers, or executives of multinational enterprises, or ministers of economy in developed countries. 'Global' here means also 'each and
everyone.' "

As Mary Ellen Holohan, SNJM, and Carroll Ann
Kemp wrote in 1980 for the National Association of
Women Religious, the Judeo-Christian tradition is calling
us as Christians, however hesitant we are to listen and to
respond, "to a posture of prophecy" and "to change."

A century after the popes first began to confront capitalist materialism (and its then parallel threat, Marxist
materialism) and a decade after Holohan and Kemp, we

still have to acknowledge that the first step has to be taken in our own everyday lives.

To battle the consumerism, in order to battle the capitalistic materialism, in order to promote economic justice, in order to witness to the cry of the poor, we still have to begin with our own search for a simple lifestyle.

We can look to, and listen to, others. But we have to begin with ourselves.

Chapter Eight

A frightening paradox lies at the heart of American and global economic life today. On the one hand, prosperity is enjoyed by the many—especially by many who happen to live in North America, Europe or Japan. In stark contrast, however, multitudes of others live in the grip of poverty—tens of millions here in the United States and nearly a billion elsewhere. Deliverance. For both rich and poor, that word may not be too strong a term to describe the national and global need.

Eighty Bishops of the
Episcopal Church, 1987

It is time now to weave. We weave together the various paths we have been taking into two major moral compass settings that merge into a single and singular direction.

Those two moral compass settings are provided by our Christian teachers, and by our own yearnings to serve and to celebrate the invitation to salvation that the good news has brought us individually.

In his 1991 letter, *Centesimus Annus*, John Paul II led off by saying that he intended to "look back, look around and look forward." So, we join him to see what specifically refers back to us as American Christians, as American Catholics.

Well, we have seen that our capitalistic, materialistic culture has played into our existing, individualistic self-love.

Such a fostering of self-love has, in turn, resulted in

shifting the entire western culture—of which the U.S. component is paramount—off track.

We can see this shift across a space of merely forty years. The U.S. diplomat, Bartley Crum, on a Middle East fact-finding tour in 1947, could genuinely defend western culture: "Westernism is not an evil. A chance for a decent life as free as possible from squalor, disease, corruption, exploitation; the 'life, liberty and the pursuit of happiness,' which we hold as inalienable rights—surely these western ideals are not evil."

Yet in 1988, a Korean lawyer could illustrate just one example of the shift when he asked: "Why do these young Koreans, unlike their parents, dislike America so intensely?" Sung-Chull Junn answered his own question: "Older Koreans grew up hearing about George Washington's cherry tree and how honesty formed the underpinnings of American society. The Puritan ethic of sexual moderation and hard work commanded respect from me and my elders. What young Koreans sees today is quite different. Soap operas broadcast by the American military television network, which a vast number of Korean students watch to learn English, contain sexual extravagance and moral deviations which directly violate the traditional morality of Koreans. News stories about homosexuality, AIDS, drugs and violent crime have tarnished America's image as a moral leader."

The western culture which Bartley Crum could defend in 1947 now represents something unacceptable; a gross overlay of permissiveness crinkle-wraps the hedonistic culture, both of them promoted by advertising, given flesh by television and marketed by unprincipled capitalism.

"The value of culture," wrote W. Somerset Maugham in *The Summing Up*, "is its effect on character. Its use is for *life*. Its aim is not beauty, but *goodness*." America, and therefore the west, is going for neither beauty nor goodness, but for success. And it has achieved one measure of it, the materialistic. But as the transplanted French writer Ted Morgan comments, "No one ever said success leads to serenity."

This materialist success was analyzed by John Paul in his observation that "the poor ask for the right to share in enjoying material goods and to make use of their capacity for work. But prosperity . . . is not only a case of raising all peoples to the level currently enjoyed by the richest countries, but rather building up a more decent life."

He again looked at why capitalism alone can never be an answer: "Of itself, an economic system does not possess criteria for correctly distinguishing new and higher forms of satisfying human needs from artificial new needs which hinder the formation of a mature personality."

John Paul reduced all these charges to a single statement, already mentioned earlier: "Poor people and poor nations—poor in different ways, not lacking food, but also deprived of freedom and other human rights—will sit in judgment on those people who take these goods away from them, amassing to themselves the imperialistic monopoly of economic and political supremacy at the expense of others."

This is our economic way and our political supremacy of which the pope speaks.

We have seen John Paul II represent what anti-Catholic writer Paul Blanshard called "the force of world Catholicism," refusing to yield an inch as John Paul and that "force" confront "the force of western culture"—capitalism. But John Paul II does not come through unscathed. He refuses to acknowledge population as an issue and, perhaps worse, gives no lead into economic change by example. He does not practice what he preaches.

In earlier writings, when he called on churches to sell

their unnecessary ornamentations and give the money to
the poor, he did not take the obvious step and look around
his own church—the Vatican—and do likewise.

When, in Yankee Stadium, he called on everyone to
give not merely of his or her affluence but also of his or
her substance, he did not give an example of how. He did
not cause those agencies over which he has the greatest
control, the Vatican and to some extent the national hier-
archies, to do as much.

What John Paul does possess, in addition to a sense of
theater, is the skills of an intellectual street fighter. He is
smart, savvy, extremely tough—and he understands
power. It is the understanding of power, the power of
world forces, that he best demonstrates in *Centesimus
Annus*, indeed in all his teaching. He understands the
power of capitalist materialism and opposes it.

He wants Catholics to use their power: he especially
wants western Catholics to exercise their power for economic change. Catholics have to try even if they fail. The
English novelist Graham Greene saw his first example of
Catholic action on a social issue—"a real attempt to put
into force the papal encyclicals which had condemned
capitalism quite as strongly as communism," he wrote—
not in Europe, but in the United States. It was 1938, and
Greene was in San Antonio, Texas and en route to Mexico
and the journey that would produce *The Power and the
Glory*. In San Antonio a Father Lopez was leading a strike
by pecan factory workers who had just had their fifty
cents a day wages cut in half.

The strike succeeded in a sense, but within months
the majority of strikers had lost their jobs because the
production line was mechanized. Nonetheless, Green did
not forget Lopez' example, and it is *example* that Christians are supposed to set when conditions demand.

A few years ago, Marvel Comics produced comic books on both John Paul and St. Francis of Assisi. In the truncated manner of comic book narrative, Pope Innocent III tells Francis: "Your ideals are some of the finest ever conceived. It grieves me to see them watered down and tampered with." John Paul II is Innocent III urging us all to be American models of Francis, combining the best American ideals with the ideals of Catholic social teaching.

This pope, as he "looks around," is also telling us that as Americans we are the richest one percent of the world, even the more modestly employed of us. But given the knowledge of modern times, something far beyond Francis' era, we have to make the connections between our wealth and the world's poverty, between our two-car family and Brazil's two million street children, between what missionary Father Joseph Donders calls the casual purchase of another compact disc and the malnutrition of a child in Nairobi's slums.

As American Christians we have to find these connections, to make them plain and understandable, to rework western life as a result and, therefore, to rework life for the world.

There *is* a connection.

So where do we begin?

Where we are.

We are the rich, all of us. Jesus warns us many times, not least in Matthew 19: "I tell you solemnly, it will be hard for a rich man to enter the kingdom of heaven. Yes, I tell you again, it is easier for a camel to pass through the eye of a needle than for a rich man to enter the kingdom of heaven." Those who heard him were astonished. Many of those who have heard John Paul II also are astonished.

And when we realize that Jesus is talking also to us, who at times might be finding it a bit hard to make ends meet, we also are astonished. But we are astonished only because we have not yet crossed the bridge from seeing our affluence as the norm to seeing poverty as the norm.

We must plunge into the work to change the poverty and let that plunging direct us. We are moving toward our neighbor, every neighbor. But something has to be happening within ourselves. We have to become ascetics. We have to learn to *deliberately* do without. And the result of that saving must be directed to helping others.

It would be arrogance to think we can do all this alone. We cannot do it alone—I almost wrote, "unarmed." We have to begin where Christianity begins, with Jesus' words and life. We do that even as we know that the secular world does not *listen* to, nor like to hear, social problems discussed in "church" talk vocabulary.

We have to accept our love relationship with Jesus: "The depth and fullness of our love of neighbor depends exclusively on our love for Jesus," wrote Dietrich von Hillebrand. Hillebrand was making us face up to the fact that death is always just ahead, and we shall not be long now in meeting up with Jesus.

What will we have to say to him?

What will he have to say to us?

Which of our neighbors will be standing alongside Jesus at that encounter? Perhaps the people who live in Bishop Pedro Casadaliga's Brazilian diocese on whose behalf Casadaliga told the world bankers—in a now justly famous quote—"[Brazil's] debt has already been collected. It was collected by taking our natural resources and cheap labor. It was collected in our infant mortality and in the blood and deaths of all our people."

This poverty is created, exacerbated, worsened because other people *want* wealth for themselves. The world is not impoverished by people who "accidentally" become wealthy—the suddenly famous pop singer, the lucky inventor, the amazing sports star. The poverty is ensured, deepened, by people for whom wealth accumulation is their ambition, their goal.

We are always and constantly in danger of forgetting what money is, what money requires, what money is for.

Here is John Wesley, preaching more than two centuries ago: "Why should you throw money upon your children any more than upon yourself—in delicate food, in gay or costly apparel, in superfluities of any kind? Why should you purchase for them more pride or lust, more vanity or foolish and hurtful desires? They do not want any more; they have enough already. Why should you be at greater expense to increase their temptations and snares, and to pierce them through with many sorrows?"

Isn't that *today*? Isn't that *now*—even though it was two centuries ago? Can't we hear Jesus echoing through Wesley's words? We really can.

Why? Because we are getting to know better, more closely and personally, those words. We have learned something after all: to turn to the scriptures and let them, in the light of this very *today*—for they will read differently tomorrow, just as they read differently yesterday—in the light of this very *today* lead us to and through *today*.

We need not concern ourselves with tomorrow's steps. Today's will give us trouble enough.

In Spiritan Fr. Father Eugene Hillman's words, we need "a willingness to take risks, with a confident faith in the Spirit." Yet we only begin with the scriptures. We must move into community for the support necessary to act. Christian life is a series of meetings in upper rooms and lower rooms and basement rooms.

There is a scene set in the very first paragraph of Ed Griffith-Nolan's book *Witness for Peace* which every

Christian knows instinctively, even when the setting is different: "On a clear fall weekend in October of 1983, I sat with two dozen other people in a room at a convent in Philadelphia. Each of us had heard disturbing reports."

Those people were concerned with disturbing reports from Nicaragua. We, here, are concerned with disturbing reports from other poor places.

But we know those little meetings, the one or two or ten percent of the community, gathered in the room where someone forgot to turn the heat or the air conditioner on soon enough, where the air is a bit stale and the room usually a bit too cavernous for the small numbers who gather.

We know we are Christians by our meeting spaces.

We are gathered because we know the difference between right and wrong and are trying to do something to change the wrong.

In our particular instance, we are gathered for support in this bold step Redmond Mullins talked about in *The Wealth of Christians*. He said that "enjoyment of the good things in life should be an aspect of the Christian's experience," yet "some form or degree of poverty is a requirement for Christians. This includes, but is more than, an internal detachment from wealth and indifference at the prospect of impoverishment, which after all were stoic requirements. It also includes a self-liberating despisal of riches, as in the cynic tradition, but without pride or contempt toward others. Poverty makes a strong demand on Christians."

Scary.

But not an impossible demand. God got us this far. God wants us to experience what it is Jesus talks about. We have to know the poor as one of us. To see the poor, in the street, or in the hovel halfway around the world, as an individual whom we know. To be able to look into those eyes and see an individual, a person. A singular person with whom contact is possible, despite social or language differences. How we then go is our decision based on our present life commitment and circumstances.

We can hesitate, but by this point we know we cannot avoid. We are down to the personal, unique to us: How?

With any luck, and just for this moment, we have been able to set aside the ego.

Oh, and our egos will be bashed and wounded. Every time we look up and see others looking at us, cynically, or with disdain, or misunderstanding—friends or family, especially. Then the ego will start urging us again to ask ourselves again on our own behalf: "What about me? When do I get mine?"

But "mine" is what capitalism is all about.

So, instead, we run to the strength of the sacraments, and we run, for we must, to the shelter of the scriptures, and we run to the support of the group, and we can then seek a little solitude in which to reflect, with ego at a safe distance, to listen internally to the Jesus who speaks to us, to me, personally and individually.

When we listen, we do hear those who can truly, in Christ's view, ask: But what about *me?* The poor. And we hear the echo from which there is no escape: "Whatever you do for these, the least of mine, you do for me."

Questions For Discussion

Chapter One

1. Close your eyes and imagine starting a business that you would really like to run. What would the business be?

2. Now, eyes open, did you start that business purely to make money, or was there equally, or predominantly, a creative element to your starting that business?

3. What do you think is a good or adequate definition of capitalism?

4. Is profit the primary goal of capitalism? If so, can capitalism be good?

5. What is the relationship of business and capitalism?

6. Can it be shown that the capitalist heritage is rooted in Scripture and/or the Judeo-Christian tradition?

7. List some of "the human inadequacies of capitalism and the resulting domination of things over people" (*Centesimus Annus*).

Chapter Two

1. Is making money Wall Street fashion, investing, "good" capitalistic creativity?

2. Can "enlightened self-interest" be a Christian principle of action?

3. Can it be moral for an entrepreneur to make an unlimited fortune meeting the need of the public?

4. Is capitalism compatible with the "common good"?

5. Explain how living out Christian ideals as a business person can be counter-cultural.

6. Which capitalism—good, bad or ugly—do you think eastern Europe and the new "Soviet" countries will actually develop?

Chapter Three

1. Is the "maximization of profits" proper only to "bad capitalism"?

2. If an owner must shut down because of lack of profit, is he required to suffer a loss on behalf of the workers?

3. Give some concrete examples of economic practices which are legal but immoral.

4. Is it possible to be a good Christian owner or executive in a "bad" or "ugly" capitalistic system? What must one do?

5. Explain why "ugly" capitalism is in reality a "sinful structure" and how it is created and developed.

6. Explain how "success" in secular life or the corporate world can be a serious risk for Christians.

Chapter Four

1. What does St. Thomas mean when he says that we should not consider our material possessions as our own but common to all?

2. As an owner of wealth, do I not have the right to hold it or dispose of it as freely as I please?

3. What do the expressions "trickle down theory" and "supply side economics" actually mean? Are they essential aspects of current capitalist theory?

4. Is government regulation compatible with capitalism? Explain.

5. Does "ugly" capitalism foster free market competition, which is supposed to be an essential aspect of our American economic system?

6. Is so-called "democratic capitalism" good capitalism or merely "insidious materialism with a Christian veneer"?

Chapter Five

1. What is materialism? Give some examples.

2. How does advertising sustain materialism?

3. Do you think the advertising industry as it exists in America is immoral?

4. List some values that are counter-cultural to the capitalist ethos.

5. Is the integral *human* development of third world nations dependent on economic development according to the capitalist model?

6. Explain how advertising is such a large part of "ugly" capitalism.

7. What is meant by a Christian counter-cultural attitude? Give examples.

8. Can enlightened self-interest be the primary principle of action in politics for a Christian?

Chapter Six

1. Do you think that the government of the United States is controlled by the wealthy?

2. What is social sin?

3. What is social justice?

4. Is it possible to transform a system of "bad" and "ugly" capitalism to "good" capitalism? How?

5. Can a national economic system be considered good or bad in itself in isolation from the world economic situation?

6. Is the disproportionate share of the world's wealth controlled by Americans immoral and unjust?

7. Explain the meaning of "the preferential option for the poor." Do you agree with it?

8. Which is primary in the U.S. government's foreign policy—economic self-interest or concerns for human rights? Explain.

9. Are we, as American Christians, guilty of the sin of being "the enemy of the poor"?

Chapter Seven

1. Can money-making be a Christian virtue or vocation?

2. If "the market be appropriately controlled by the forces of society and by the state" (*Centesimus Annus*), is this capitalism?

3. Are producers' cooperatives and worker-owned industries models of "good" capitalism?

4. In the United States we understand and practice political democracy. Could a Christian strategy for change be to find ways of extending this democratic process from the political to the economic sphere?

5. Can alternatives to "ugly" capitalism be found on the capitalist's terms?

6. What is the solution to "ugly" capitalism, or plutarchy? Government control? Democratic capitalism? Democratic socialism?

7. Pope John Paul II demands "that the market be appropriately controlled by the forces of society and by the state" to "guarantee that the basic needs of the whole of society are satisfied." Is this not a principle acceptable to socialism and anathema to capitalism?

Chapter Eight

1. Does any economic system have within itself its own criteria of correction, or must it be judged and directed by moral and cultural values outside itself? Explain.

2. Does the United States control the world by its de facto economic might and political supremacy? Give examples.

3. If the Catholic Church were to divest itself of all signs of apparent affluence and give the money to the poor, would this be only a fruitless symbolic act or would it be a really helpful lead to economic change by way of good example?

4. Explain some practical ways in which poverty must be an essential ingredient in the lives of first world Christians.